Self-publishing Unboxed

The Three-year, No-bestseller Plan For
Making A Sustainable Living From Your Fiction

Book 1

Print Edition

Cover design by Patty Jansen

Sign up to be notified of new works by this
author: http://pattyjansen.com

Contents

This Is A Book About Making Money From Your Writing

GASP, I KNOW. How dare I talk about money?

Writers are supposed to be precious and exclusive creatures who need no food and clothing and have no kids who need education and no rent that needs paying. They live off thin air. They have no lives because they can't afford lives, begging from friends, couch-surfing, slaving away in exploitative, backbreaking jobs, all the while banging away at their typewriters in the attic at night.

Because, art.

Every now and then, you will come across much-hyped articles in lauded, old-fashioned newspapers, or even websites (but writers can't afford the Internet, remember?) that perpetuate the myth of a poor suffering writer by trotting out just one of these writers.

They signed a book deal, got a $3000 advance. The book never earned out, and the publisher didn't want the second book. They wrote another book that sold even less and now earn a pittance from their writing and supplement their writing income from speaking gigs and teaching writing classes. Because, obviously, the world needs more starving writers who can't sell their books.

I know, right?

Of course, on the other side we find the other myth, that of the writer selling their soul to the devil called commerce, writing vast quantities of pulp books, churning them out, even contracting other people to write for them, because they write books that readers gobble up like cheap candy. This soulless writing (or so the literati say) thrives on churn; one book is like every other. But, hey, at least these writers can afford to pay for their own attic.

Stereotypes. Who doesn't love them? As soon as you say you're a writer, people will mentally put you in either of those two boxes.

This book is not about either of those extremes, although both definitely exist. It is also not about the soulless grind of finding an agent and selling your book to publishers who pay next to nothing, make you sign restrictive contracts, give you a poor cover and publish the book two years after they acquired it, barely market it and then hog your rights until the end of time.

It's about writing what you love, writing it well, positioning it well in today's market, and building a sustainable long term income through taking control of your own publication and your own audience.

It's a book about making a viable, sustainable income through self-publishing.

A lot of writers are doing this already. They are not writers you will find mentioned in articles in *The Guardian*, because they don't have spectacular multi-million bestseller success. They are not the Amanda Hockings and Hugh Howeys and Andy Weirs of the world, although all of those saw fame from self-published books. But many of the writers I'm talking about never have any books in any top 100 anywhere.

They are writers who have been empowered by the ability to upload their own books to retailers and cut out the necessity of a middleman, a.k.a a publisher. They have done this by putting out quality books that enough readers wanted to read that they, the authors, could lead the lives they have always dreamed of.

Self-publishing has changed the lives of many. It has enabled carers to look after their sick partners, parents to be there for their kids, retirees to travel around the world or simply live comfortably. It's allowed people to leave toxic marriages, leave bad jobs, provide for disabled family members, pay off mortgages, or even obtain mortgages.

It involves nothing except yourself, your sense of savvy and your computer.

It's self-publishing, but self-publishing with a plan.

But first . . .

Self-Publishing Unboxed

FIRST WE NEED to put a few myths to sleep that still circulate about self-publishing, myths that have proven very hard to kill.

The myth that all self-published books are crap

There is certainly a lot of crap out there. Self-published authors are not helping by putting out poorly written books with zero editing. And by poorly written, I don't mean books that don't conform to some literati's self-imposed high standard of crafted prose, I mean books with such poor and twisted sentences that they are barely readable. Books with so many demonstrable grammar and spelling errors that a primary school kid with a decent grasp of language could do better. Unedited books by people who obviously don't write a lot in English, or books that have been hauled through Google Translate. Books with extremely badly made pixelated covers. Books with formatting that renders them unreadable.

I mean books that fail the absolute minimum standards of publication.

And the fact that this myth exists is because there are still far too many people out there putting out books just like that. So maybe "self-published books are crap" is not a myth, but it's definitely a myth when you want to apply it to all self-published books.

The thing is, there are also a lot of books that look great, contain fewer editing oopsies than books from big publishers, and have awesome covers. Books that look indistinguishable from trade-published books. Books that have been through a thorough editing process, have a professional cover, and have been formatted by a professional.

If you're still doubtful that such books exist, go to the Science Fiction > Space Opera category on Amazon US, and look at the publishers of the bestselling books. If it says "Amazon Digital Editions" or the book is in Kindle Unlimited, then it's self-published. On non-Amazon retailers, it will often say Smashwords Edition, or the publisher may be listed as Draft2Digital. At the time of writing, trade publishers appear to have withdrawn from publishing Space Opera. Self-published writers OWN this category on all platforms.

These quality books are the books we're talking about. These are the books we want to emulate.

The myth that self-published books sell a hundred copies at best

Here is a chart for you. It's boiled down from a chart made by a writing friend of mine, data geek Phoenix Sullivan, who is a consultant for the Author Earnings reporting site. If you've never visited Author Earnings nor seen their awesome quarterly reports, click that link and go there now. Never mind this book. It will still be here when you come back.

The basis for the Author Earnings reports is an extended version of this table:

Ranking on Amazon US	Copies sold in previous 24h to obtain rank
1	7000
4	5500
20	3000
100	1100
200	600
1500	100
3000	70
10,000	13
50,000	3
100,000	1

Number of copies sold to obtain a certain ranking on Amazon (source: Phoenix Sullivan)

Now, using the parameters I gave earlier to determine which books are self-published, have a look at the top 100 books in your favourite genre and find some self-published books. See how many copies these books sell per day. This is just section—namely Amazon US—of ONE retailer. There are other Amazon stores and there are other retailers.

Case closed.

Of course we cannot all sell this many copies, but there are good sales to be made without ever hitting the top 100 in any genre. In fact, there is a good living to be made from selling 1 copy a day of each of your twelve books on multiple retailers.

But if anyone tells you, "Self-published books don't sell," tell them that well-edited, well-produced self-published books not only sell, they allow the writers to quit their day jobs. And show them the current Amazon bestseller lists for each genre and then that table.

Obviously, putting out a well-produced book and marketing it well is the holy grail. This book is about that. But first . . .

Put On Your Snark And Distrust

WHEN YOU HAVE decided to self-publish, your wallet becomes a battleground.

Sharks start circling the moment you utter the word "self-publishing". Self-publishing means that you'll need to contract out some tasks, notably those you can't do yourself. These are tasks like editing, because it's extremely hard to spot your own errors, and cover design, because you don't have an artistic bone in your body. Don't get me wrong, these are good expenses. But there are also many potential pitfalls, money-wasters and outright scams.

The big sharks

Start by googling "self-publishing" for example. What comes up? A whole page of vanity presses!

These "companies" (I prefer to use the word scammers) prey on the insecurity of hopeful writers. Those people want to self-publish, but have no idea how. Mostly, they have a long list of rejections from traditional publishers (and, sadly, often with reason), have been worn out by the grind and have decided to do it themselves. They start by doing the one thing that would normally give you some pretty decent answers: googling.

Nope! The vanity presses have hijacked the google search results. Not only that, but these results will keep following you around the Internet for the next few months in the Google Ads boxes. Just waiting for you to say: I looked at all the advice, but all this talk about formatting and finding an editor and marketing is too hard, why don't I pay someone $10,000 and be done with it all. Why wouldn't you? Because you're retired, and you have $10,000, and you understand and accept that everything costs money. It's rather a bit more than you expected to pay, but hey, you get to see your book published, and look! They offer publicity packages as well!

All of this would be fine, if all these "publishers" did was provide you with the services, and did a decent job. But no—the services I've seen rendered by them are second-rate, overpriced and sometimes unnecessary or ineffective. I've even seen press releases and book launches included in the pricing models!

For those who think a book launch party is vital, understand that the book launch is usually put on by a big publisher. The customers of Big Publishing are bookshops, and bookshop managers like coming to these after-work shindigs so that they can socialise. It has little to do with selling books to readers.

But, worse than all of this, the vanity presses sell you hope.

They sell you the idea that everything will be taken care of, and that their expensive "publicity" package actually includes things that work. They sell you the idea that they will take care of the publishing (which they do, overpriced and second-rate though it usually is) and that they will deal with the marketing. Because it's the thought of marketing that will give many writers nightmares. They don't want to do the marketing. But, get this: every writer needs to do marketing. Even if you get a traditional publishing deal with a big publisher, you will have to do marketing. If you don't, the publisher won't sign your next book, because you won't sell very many. Marketing is a thing that you do every day.

The days that publishers did this all for you and all you needed to do was write in your attic are over. Done. Finished. Dead as a dodo.

So, get used to it: market or die.

YOU do the marketing. Not some company. Definitely not some company you paid $10,000 to publish your book, because here is another thing about these scammers: once your book is out the door, they're done with you. They've delivered what they said they would: editing (that leaves much to be desired), a cover (which is usually acceptable) and marketing package (that consists of press releases and other crap that doesn't work but sounds really nice).

They're done with you, and you have boxes of books in your garage with no idea how to sell them, and they have gone in search of the next sucker to milk.

If you're still dubious, it is worth noting that people who publish through vanity presses are often attached to the "old ways". They want to get into bookshops and see their books on the shelves. How ironic it is, then, that bookshops are more likely to stock a book openly self-published through Createspace (Amazon's self-publishing Print-On-Demand arm) than one published through one of these predatory companies. And while we're at it, promotional sites are not going to want your book either. Don't. Just don't waste your money. Spend it on learning to write engaging stories.

Not having $10,000 to spend can be a blessing in disguise. Money is definitely no substitute for a bit of common sense, and "having more money than brains" is a real thing. Don't be one of those people.

The little sharks

Say you've managed to avoid the vanity presses and you have found the real self-publishing crowd. Know that sharks are still common.

There are contractors who will take your money and won't deliver, promotional sites that will use shady tactics to promote your book (clickfarms, incentivised buys, buy circles) that can get you into trouble with the retailers and can get your accounts on those retailers suspended. Others will simply try to sell you things you don't need or charge you a lot of money for promotions that don't work.

So you must develop a strong sense of distrust. But, I can hear you say, I know little, how do I find out whether a service is legit, whether I need that service or if it's any good?

Google is usually your friend here, especially in terms of reviews of business services, but the best method I recommend is to become part of a self-publishing community. The strongest and most ethical and on-the-ball community is the Writer's Cafe at the Kindleboards. If you have a question about self-publishing, ask it there. This includes questions about paid services, whether they're any good, whether you need them or whether cheaper options are available.

The forum can be a bit snarky if members feel a certain service or reply doesn't pass muster, but developing a good sense of distrust and snark is vital in this business.

Also check Writer Beware and the attached blog.

What about the plethora of courses?

It has become extremely popular for everyone who is in the writing/teaching business to bring out an online course. Are these the real deal or not?

You need to know two things about these courses:

1.   These courses contain nothing that you can't find out online. If the course teacher claims there is, don't take the course. It's highly likely to be against someone's terms of service.

2.   These courses help you to find this material quickly, and they connect you with a community. Especially the latter can be extremely valuable if you're not already part of a community. A course can be a short-cut.

Before you sign up for a course, determine what it teaches. The more specific, the better. Determine that this is a subject that you need to learn about and, more importantly, that you're willing to invest time and money into learning. There is no point in taking a course and then being hesitant to invest in buying and using the software, memberships, ad platforms or other things that were taught in the course.

Don't forget to evaluate the credentials of the people giving the course. Don't just look at testimonials, but look at the course provider's style and whether that suits your own style. Often these course providers put out a plethora of free webinars, where you can get a glimpse of the type of person giving the course. Don't buy a course unless you can get a glimpse into what it looks like. The best course providers give out a lot of material for free so that you can judge their style before parting with money.

On the subject of money, make sure there is a refund policy.

And decide whether you want to fork out the money and fast-track your learning or whether you have the time to learn organically online. I'm not advocating one over the other. It's up to you to decide. You're going to hear this line a lot in this book. It's not called self-publishing for nothing.

Shark-repellent

Unfortunately, when it comes to paid services, you need to be vigilant. If you adhere to these few guidelines, you'll potentially save yourself a lot of heartache and money.

♦   When something sounds too good to be true, it always is. Not just that, but Amazon is likely to ban your seller's account over it.

♦   In relation to the above, if someone tells you about a

magic promotion and won't be up-front about how it is done, show you where the book will be promoted and how readers can sign up, then RUN! Chances are high that something shady is being done.

◆   NOBODY can guarantee a certain number of sales or downloads. If they do, they're using clickfarms to artificially boost your rankings. RUN!

◆   When someone cold-contacts you and wants to offer something that you need to pay for, it's never something you want.

◆   When someone gives you advice about how to sell and they don't actually, you know, appear sell a decent number of books or have a history of selling in the genre you want to write in, then what is that advice worth? Repeat with any other service that deals with the production or selling of books.

◆   On the flip side of the above, if someone sells really well, how much of that is going to be a product of their unique history, a history you don't share? Maybe they got a special opportunity years ago that is not applicable for you now. In particular, the advice of people who "made it" years ago may be outdated, because they are not familiar with what it's like to start as a new author now. They are also likely to give you marketing advice that's in line with their much larger budget and tolerance for risk.

◆   You should always evaluate marketing advice given against your situation and make your own decisions. It doesn't mean the other person is wrong, but their marketing advice might not be right for you.

- ◆ On the other hand, if someone who sells well gives you advice about your product, then do listen carefully.

- ◆ No one will care more about your books than you will. Don't believe anyone who makes wonderful promises, for example a certain number of sales. People look after number one. Fact of life.

- ◆ And with all the above rules, remember this: never, ever leave your brain at home, and always carry a bullshit meter. Your gut is always right. If it smells like a fart that is because is it a fart.

- ◆ And if in doubt, ask the Writer's Cafe at the Kindleboards. You will not find a bunch of people who are more apt at poking holes in some service provider's promises anywhere on the Internet.

There's sharks in them thar waters. This book is your harpoon. (Sorry, I love bad metaphors.)

With this said, we will now move into the most important part of the plan. No, grasshopper, this is not the nuts and bolts of how to set up your mailing list. It's about more stuff you don't want to read.

Why You Don't Want To Read This Book

IF THIS WERE a book of the how-to variety, this would be the part where the cheery recommendations go.

You know the shtick. So-and-so big name writer tried my method and had instant success, increasing sales by fifty percent.

Except this book is not about that. Not that people don't do well following the three-year plan mindset, and many others like it. To the contrary. There is a whole host of writers making a good living following methods like these.

It's just that the three-year plan is not a box of tricks. This book is not about the glamour or the magic pill. It's about putting the many moving parts of your author business together.

The three-year plan is a philosophy that serves both as sales vehicle and as attitude check to keep you happy and avoid burnout. The three-year plan relies on consistency and persistence more than quote-worthy immediate success. This is not a paint-by-numbers book. It is about writing what you want to write and marketing it.

Massive success is fickle. It frequently comes when you're not ready for it. For a host of reasons, it is rarely sustainable. It's certainly not wise to suggest that it's a right to be earned and kept forever.

What goes up must come down, nothing lasts forever, and other bad clichés. They're clichés because they are true.

Writing income needs to be managed, the troughs ironed out, the peaks savoured, money squirrelled away, because income is neither regular nor secure. It's the nature of the beast.

Rather than telling you all kinds of wonderful things about this book and why you have to read it, I will tell you that you shouldn't read it. You shouldn't read it because it won't tell you what you want to hear: that publishing is easy, that you will make a million dollars in your first year or that your books will be an instant success if only you follow these easy steps.

Make no mistake, having a career as a writer is hard.

But having a career in writing is also much more achievable than it has ever been before. There are many writers making decent money selling ebooks, people you will never have heard of. People selling enough books to pay some or all of their bills.

This book will show you how to have a rewarding career that

will build your reader base. This book will show you how to sustain sales in between releases and promotions and other slow periods. This book will show you how to be independent of sales platforms and algorithms and how to spend more of your time doing what you enjoy: writing.

The Plan On Steroids

FOR THOSE KEEN to get into it, here is the plan in the form in which it was originally published as post on the Kindleboards forum. If you decide to take control over your own publishing efforts and are not on the Kindleboards yet, you should join right now. In fact, go and do it before you forget. This book will still be here when you come back.

Like most large forums, the place can be a bit confusing and knives can and do come out, but in general it's a friendly place where you will meet many other writers and find advice, especially if you're just starting out.

The post is quoted here because it still gets a lot of visits. People will read this and will recognise it. Many people have asked me to expand on the different aspects that make up the plan.

The Three-Year, No-bestseller Plan To Making A Sustainable Income From Your Writing

Part 1: the product

1. Write a series of three books in a genre you like. It's best if the books are full-length of 70-80k words at least. There are people who can get away with novellas, but selling well gets harder the shorter your books are. Unless, maybe, your genre is erotica or romance. Maybe. Just make the books full-length, OK? It makes life so much easier (insert whisper that sounds like Bookbub: many advertising sites don't accept short books).

2. Make the first book free.

3. Play around a bit with advertising, if you feel so inclined (I mean—why the hell not?), but don't worry about stuff that takes you away from writing too much.

4. Make sure you have the following in all your books: a link to your mailing list signup form, and, at the end, a live link to the next book in the series.

5. When you finish the series, or even while you're writing it, start the next series. Make it a slightly different subgenre, or use a different setting and characters. Make sure that people don't need to have read the other series in order to follow it. Write three books. Make the first book free.

6. Repeat 5. Twice, if you can. Three years @ 4 novels a year = 12 books = 4 trilogies.

7. Advertise your freebies, but don't fall down any rabbit holes that take you away from writing for major chunks of time (insert snort that sounds like Facebook advertising).

Part 2: the marketing

1. After a while, your mailing list will start to build up a bit (see point 4 above). Get a paid account at MailChimp or wherever you are. If you are not at a list provider that allows automation and segmentation, and most importantly, automation based on automatic segmentation, move your list.

2. Set up mailing automation. When people join your list, send them an email with the freebies, even though they're already free. Don't email the freebies to them, but include download links in the email. Then booby-trap those links so that you can track who downloads what. You'll be using this later.

3. Next, send your subscribers to an automated program that sends them something at regular intervals (Amazon genre newsletters arrive every two weeks, that's good enough for me). What do you write about? About you, about your fiction, free short stories, you ask them questions, tell them about tidbits of research you've done, or places you travelled for your writing. Tell them about box sets you're in, and even plug your friends with similar books. Anything. Booby-trap any links to your books so your MailChimp/AWeber/whatever account knows who clicked what.

4. Siphon people who clicked all the links to series 1

(and downloaded the freebie!) off to a side list, and say three months later send them an email saying: hey, this is book 2 in the series. Do this with all books 2 in all your series.

5. Repeat steps 3 and 4. Create new emails, use the links and who clicks them to segment your list and send them further information based on who clicked what.

6. Pronto! You have now created your own marketing machine that crawls like a giant slug over your sub-scriber list.

Part 3: your tasks

It's now really clear what you need to do:

1. Keep writing new books that people want to read, continuing your most popular series, starting new series maybe (make book 1 free again). Add new emails about those books to your mailing sequence.

2. Keep feeding people into your giant mailing slug.

There you go. This is the basis of the plan.

Note that there are certain things I don't do anymore, for example, my automation is much simplified. If you move your list to another mailing list provider, or the provider changes their automation process—two things that happened to me in close succession—this badly stuffs up your process. Much better to have a simple sequence that you can quickly rebuild from scratch.

Also, I quite enjoy manually emailing people every two weeks and including recent news. These emails have taken the place of blog posts.

My books are also no longer free on the retailer sites. Instead people can download them for free from Instafreebie in exchange for their email address. Instafreebie feeds them directly into my automation sequence.

Don't worry if this went over your head. In the rest of the book, we go into details about how to set all this up.

But first: none of this will work without some more stuff you don't want to hear about.

This Is The Part You Really Don't Want To Read

NONE OF THE PLAN outlined in this book will work if you don't have a book people want to read.

Let's just repeat that:

You must have a book people want to read.

Sorry to put a damper on your enthusiasm, but you need to learn to write well before you can learn to sell.

This is not a writing craft book, and most of this book is written under the assumption that you have done this, that you have read about story structure and plot and have done a class or two, or spent some time in writing workshops or have otherwise honed your craft.

Some people are natural learners and absorb craft through reading in the genre they want to write in.

But the truth is, just like you can't pick up an instrument and get a gig in a professional orchestra, everyone has to learn to write.

On top of that, once you have written well, everyone needs to learn how to present their book and make it the best possible product before you can start marketing it. Otherwise there is absolutely no point in doing all the other work.

It Starts And Ends With The Book

IT SHOULDN'T NEED to be said, but the most important thing you can do as writer is to write a good book.

Really.

In the marketing hype, this simple fact sometimes gets lost, or it gets confused with the erroneous assumption that all books are equal.

We all know they are not. We all know of good books and bad books. If pressured, most of us will even realise that our good books are not the same as someone else's good books. There is a name for people who don't realise this: it's "literary snobs".

Another truth is that every book will find someone who loves it, even if it's only the writer's mother.

The trick is writing a book that appeals to enough people for it to be marketable. It doesn't need to be a mega-bestseller. The key is enough people.

How do you know if your book is marketable?

If you have published your book, and people buy it who are not your friends and family, and if people regularly continue to buy it when you promote, you probably have a marketable book or at least the seeds of a marketable book.

If you run promotions or make your book free, and many people download it, but you're having trouble selling book 2, you might have a problem.

I'm not of the type that I'll tell you that a series should see a certain percentage of people who buy book 1 also buy book 2. This will depend on many things: the size of the promotion you have done, the size of your book, whether your audience are fast readers, whether book 1 ends in a cliffhanger, whether you can read book 2 independently and a whole bunch of other factors. It also varies over time.

But if you're unhappy with the sell-through, you can probably improve it. And you probably should improve it before you spend too much time and money on marketing.

How do you do this?

Apart from the lack of sell-through, problems in the book may manifest in the reviews. If a decent number of reviews mention that the book is slow, hard to understand, or has other problems like poor editing, then this is probably true.

In that case, fix the problems before you go any further. Definitely fix them before you spend huge amounts of money on marketing. The copies you sell or give out will be in circulation forever, and reviews about problems may turn up years after the sale of the book.

The best thing to do of course is not to publish a book with major problems in the first place.

How do you avoid publishing a book with problems?

In the first place: learn to write. I cannot stress this enough, even if it is something people seem to want to hear the least.

Spend time doing this. Not months, years. Take some courses, read some books. Join some writing communities and then submit to agents and publishers. No, not because self-publishing is second best, only to be considered if you can't get a traditional deal. It is because for all the supposed ills of the publishing industry, it is still full of people who love books and who see a lot of books pass their desk and who can spot a book that's well-written—even if it may not be up their alley. They will tell you so in their rejection letters: "This is well-written, but doesn't fit our catalogue."

Submit books to them until you get these types of personal replies. Submit shorter works to magazines. Publish a few. Get a sense of confidence that you can write a decent story with a beginning, middle and end in language that a lot of people find pleasant to read.

Seriously: learn to write.

As a caution, don't confuse "quality" with spelling and grammar issues, or with adherence to the many self-imposed "writing rules" that circulate around the learn-to-write community.

Some writers genuinely believe their manuscript will be publishable, if only they eradicate every instance of "that" from their manuscripts. Or if they use no "passive voice" (and then they get confused about what passive voice actually is). Remember that there is only one thing worse than a piece of fiction where the word "was" is used multiple times in a sentence: one that has been contorted so that it doesn't occur at all.

If someone says your fiction has a stylistic issue, like the overuse of certain words or constructions, then (presuming the construction you used is grammatically correct), removing and fixing half of them is sufficient to get rid of the problem.

The writing rules are not silly and stupid, as some say. Religious adherence to them, is.

The rules were created with the purpose of making your book more readable. Ultimately, all of them serve the following purposes:

◆   Don't bore the reader

◆   Don't confuse the reader

◆   Don't annoy the reader.

All the rules are mere crutches to aid those points. Don't be boring, don't be confusing, don't be annoying. That's it.

But much more important than all this nitty-gritty is the story. This is why you will see books which are stylistically poor, and some that even have many avoidable grammatical errors, do well: because they tell an engaging story to an audience that's looking for those stories.

Hone your craft of storytelling more than your prose-craft. This can be really hard. It can lead to having to completely change your writing process. It may require help from outside.

When you have finished writing, you're not done. Once you have written, you must edit. If you think you can self-edit, think again. If you can't afford to pay for editing, at the very least get a nitpicky friend or two to read it for you. The only problem is that you are likely to have to do something for your friend in return. Or you may be able to buy their favour in cases of beer. At any rate, editing will cost you something. It could be money, it could be something else, but you need someone else to look at your work because you get sick of looking at your own words and miss the errors.

Editing

Once you decide to pay for editing—and I think it's one of the first things you should pay for as soon as you can afford it—you need to know that there are many different kinds of editing.

Developmental Editor. When you're just starting out, it may be a good idea, at least once, to get a developmental editor. This is someone who will comment on storyline, character and plot. This person will look at the flow of the story and make suggestions to have it flow better. A developmental editor is not cheap, but will absolutely make you a better writer. They may not fix that book, but will have taught you skills for future books. See it as an investment in your craft.

Content Editor. A content editor will look at the data in the book: the setting if it exists, the science if there is any, the believability and consistency of the setting. The content editor and developmental editor are often the same.

Copyeditor. A copyeditor will look at paragraphs and sentence flow.

Proofreader. This person will pick out the typos, the missed punctuation and wrongly used words. Proofreading and copyediting are the absolute bare minimum of editing you should get.

It is possible to get someone who does more than one type of editing. Definitely ask your potential editor what sort of editing they provide and what other services you should consider hiring that they don't cover.

But remember that editing enhances a work. An editor doesn't exist to fix all your problems. In fact, if a book has so many problems that it needs serious fixing, any editor worth their reputation will not take it on. If you're asking for proofreading, but what you need is extensive developmental and style editing, they will tell you so. Listen to them.

Once you have done all this, have confidence in your abilities. Even if you have edited extensively, there will almost always be some errors.

Some people will complain loudly about them, and many times these people will be wrong. If you are like me and write in Commonwealth English, readers will complain of errors, even if they mean that there is a u in colour and they're not expecting one.

People will complain. That's a fact of life. When you put something out in the world, some people will hate it. But if you've done your job, there will only be a few of these people. Don't give readers any more reason to complain than necessary. But also accept that nothing will ever be to everyone's liking.

How do you find an editor?

First, establish what kind of editing you want and look around with that in mind.

The best way is to ask for recommendations in places where self-published writers you respect hang out. You don't know any self-published writers? Get to know some already! Being part of the community is very important, I would say absolutely vital, to your career. The Kindleboards, which I've already mentioned a few times, is a great place for the purpose of finding good, reasonably-priced and reliable service providers.

Every one of my books has two editors: first I use someone who reads the books and makes suggestions regarding characters, logic and storyline. She points out the saggy bits, the rushed bits, and the parts that are unclear. We will talk about characters and whether their motivations are clear and whether or not it was clear why the characters decided to do as they did in the book.

She often tells me nothing I didn't already know or suspect, but the value in our interactions is in discussing what to do about those issues.

After this process is completed and I have done an edit, the book will go to a traditional editor who does a line-editing pass and a proofreading pass.

While you don't have to do exactly the same thing, it is a very good idea to have someone read the book for strange jumps of logic or things that may trip readers up, such as a character doing something that people would perceive as unsympathetic or dumb.

Then the copy editing step puts the final touches on the work.

But even before you get to this stage . . .

Don't Hate The Pigeonholes

A VERY IMPORTANT step in the publishing process, preferably done before you even start writing, is to determine what genre you want to market the book in.

At this point, a lot of inexperienced writers will complain that they don't like being pigeonholed. They don't like to be confined to a certain genre, or they haven't even thought about it. They wrote a mishmash of science fiction with fantasy elements, but it's set in medieval times and oh, the main character is ten, but it's definitely not a book for children. It defies classification.

This was why they got into self-publishing in the first place, right?

Well, no.

Genres are not about pigeonholes or conformity. They are

about reader expectations.

How?

Think about what you read and why you read what you read. Chances are that you read only a couple of genres. You are attracted to certain elements—or tropes—common to those genres. I like science fiction and fantasy. Tropes common to these genres are: worldbuilding, usually some sort of adventure, magic or technology that doesn't yet exist. The story is usually, but not always, told in a setting that is not today's world, or if the setting is today's world, there is usually a kind of shadow secret society.

All science fiction and fantasy includes elements that are not real and those elements are important in the story. That is the very essence of those genres. I'd be annoyed if I read a book that was just about characters in a family and might be set in the future but the setting sounds just like today and the characters don't interact with the setting. Because it wouldn't be science fiction.

Similarly, all romances include a couple, and they have a happy ending. That is the very essence of the genre. The couple can be rich, poor, from all corners of the world including the past, including the future, but the relationship between them is central and is the main driver of the plot.

In mystery and crime, the protagonist solves a problem. It could be a murder, a missing-person case, a jewel theft or something strange that happened in the local history museum. But something needs to be solved. A mystery is not about the romance between two of the characters.

These are broad expectations of genre, and as writer, you ignore them at your peril.

Consider your book in terms of these genres, so that you can give the readers what they expect to get. It is best to do this before you start writing so that you can gear your book towards those expectations. It is best to build it into the blurb—which I also recommend you write before the story.

Sure, there are books that can comfortably fit into more than one genre. In that case, you choose the one you think is most attractive to readers. Genre classification is not static and you can change it later.

If you have no idea how to classify your book, I would suggest that you read some of the bestselling books in the genres the book might fall in. And then read the blurbs of a good many more. Make notes of tone, subject matter and types of characters that you might find in titles that sell well today.

I'm afraid I'd have to say that in at least half the cases where writers aren't sure what genre to put their book in, it means they are unfamiliar with the recent publications in that genre. It often means that they've been writing on an island, with little knowledge of what's hot and what's not. It's a mark of inexperience and does not usually bode very well for the book. Sadly, Chosen One fantasy went out of fashion thirty years ago, and the readers are not terribly fond of Mary Sues either. Yet we have all innocently written those types of books—present company included. Educate yourself so that you can see that those types of stories should remain where they are: in your bottom drawer. At least until you gut the plot and turn it into a book that's more in line with what readers want today.

Yes, you can publish—that's the freedom of self-publishing—but the premise of this book was that you want to make money with your writing, so that's what I'm going to assume you want to do.

To sum up, the foremost issue is to determine what genre you book is. It doesn't matter so much that it's not a perfect fit. In fact most books can be classified in more than one way. But classified they must be, so that a reader wanting a romance gets a romance and a reader wanting a mystery gets a mystery.

Genre classification is also very important for cover design. Your cover must reflect the correct genre.

Which brings me to . . .

Everyone Judges A Book By The Cover

BECAUSE EVERYBODY DOES. Don't let anyone tell you otherwise. People judge books by their covers all the time.

If you saw a book in a bookstore with an embarrassingly hideous cover, you'd think twice about buying it. You would not want to be seen dead reading a book with that cover on public transport. Why do you think erotic fiction took off with the advent of ereaders? Because no one can see what you're reading!

That's right. People judge people by the books they're reading. People judge themselves by the covers of the books they read.

Before you upload your homemade cover, be honest about it. Do you have any graphic skills? Have you studied book covers in your genre and do you understand what makes them work?

If the answer to both is yes, go ahead and design your own cover. It is entirely possible to produce a cover that sells.

However, unless you have graphic and artistic skills, and you're aware of genre conventions and know about fonts and text placement, and have an artistic eye, and some experience, it's highly unlikely that you can design a cover that's even remotely adequate.

So, be honest: does the cover you've designed—and that looks pretty to you—look anywhere near the covers of books in your genre that sell well?

If in doubt, ask some people who read a lot of books. After all, they won't want to be seen dead with a book that has an ugly cover. Don't take their "it's not too bad" replies as encouragement. The cover you made for your first ever book is terrible. You know it.

Get a cover designer. You'll be glad that you did.

How do you find a cover designer?

Same place you find an editor: recommendations from friends and forums. There are a number of very good cover designers out there who do very nice work for not very much. As a ballpark figure, you can get a good pre-made cover starting at about $50. In case you don't know what it is, a pre-made cover is a fully designed cover where the only thing you get to change is the title and your name. This is a very good and affordable way of getting an attractive cover. No, it won't fit the book to a T, but this is much less important than authors think. The function of the book cover is to be attractive, to make people curious and inform them what sort of book they're going to get.

If you have zero graphic skills and not much money, get a pre-made cover. Don't be precious about how well it reflects the exact content of your book. Don't let an ugly or ineffective cover stand in the way of people buying your book.

If you want to move up-market, custom-made covers from reputable designers start at about $200. If you're really lucky, you can find a good designer who does it for less, but if such a person is a professional, they will be forced to charge at least that much unless design is a hobby for them.

Top-end covers should cost anywhere from $400 for photo-manipulation to $800 for hand-drawn covers. There is absolutely no need to pay more than that.

But there are a couple of important things to know when commissioning a book cover.

A cover is an image that represents the content of the book.

Above all, the cover should make it clear what genre and subgenre the book is. How do you know what this looks like? Well, go to the website of any book retailer and look at the covers of recently published book in your genre. At the moment, you will usually find dark blue covers with purples and reds with a woman in dark clothing on Urban Fantasy; you will often find a cloaked figure in a mountainous landscape in Epic Fantasy, space ships in Space Opera, a couple or just a woman with pretty colours in Romance. You'll often find an image with bold type for crime and a cover showing some object in Mystery.

Not sure about your book's genre? Go back to the previous section. You will now see that this is really important.

Apart from indicating subgenre, a good cover illustrates mood and elements from the book. Are there werewolves? Put a wolf on the cover. Does the book contain a crime? Put someone holding a gun on the cover. Add elements of setting—urban vs. country—or climate—make sure people wear thick coats.

One thing that usually does NOT make a good cover is an illustration of a scene from the book. In the vast majority of cases this is because book scenes don't convey genre, and they are often too complex and difficult to get right. For the designer—whose job it is to design your cover, not to read your book—these types of scenes and authors who insist on them are a royal pain in the butt. Authors can get way too precious about it, insist on changes that ruin the design and are outside the skill set of the designer, and the chance that whole thing ends in tears, with a poor cover, is high. A good designer will have a point where they are forced to ditch a client who is too demanding. A good designer has the reputation because their covers are good. It means they're busy. They need to deliver the goods on time. Be clear in what you want, and be reasonable. Give a designer a general brief with the sort of book it is, the elements that are in it, and a few examples of covers that you like. Especially the latter is very helpful for the designer.

And then, for Pete's sake, let the designer do their job. It's your job to write the book. It's their job to produce a cover that sells. You wouldn't want them to do your job, so don't try to do theirs.

You've got other work to do . . .

The Most Important 100 Words You'll Write

THE BLURB, or sales copy, is the most important piece of text you will write for your book. The blurb is the bit that goes on the back of a print book and in the description on retailer sites. To many writers, the blurb comes as an afterthought, but it's a vital piece of text.

In the space of a hundred words, you have to convince someone that your book is worth reading. You have to tell them about the characters and the story and make them interested in what happens.

Yet many blurbs are boring or confusing. They try to cram too much information into a small piece of text, and the end result is a paragraph or two of indigestible, confusing mush.

What goes into a good blurb?

As with most things, simple is better. A good blurb needs to be easy to understand and needs to be an engaging piece of text.

Typically it will set the scene for the story; it will introduce a main character and his or her main problems; it will state what gets in the character's way and will leave off there. The blurb is a teaser. It's meant to make you excited or curious so that you have to buy the book to find out what happens. Or it has to make you want to read about this really cool world, or it confirms that yes, this book is a proper murder mystery and therefore you'll like it if you read murder mysteries.

A typical blurb conveys genre and gives a concept, it gives an interesting problem and confirms that the problem fits within the genre, and it brings something that is unique to the book.

Make no mistake, writing a blurb is extremely hard and many writers take a long time to master it.

Some hire someone to do it for them.

There are many different styles of successful blurbs. If you want to know more about blurbs, do the one thing I have now told you to do a few times already: go to the retailer pages of your favourite genre and pull up some of the books that are similar to yours. Look at their blurbs.

A very basic example:

Johnny is an orc, but he's a smart orc and he wants to go to university. Unfortunately, the university admission criteria does not admit orcs, and the evil Dean, Dr Foster, will not make an exception. He hates orcs. But there is that science show competition that allows the winner to be accepted in the course of their choice . . .

The *concept* is: orcs going to university. This alone may make you think "Cool!"

The *character* is Johnny, who is clearly a sympathetic orc.

The *conflict* is between Johnny and Dr Foster.

The *plot* is obviously going to be about winning the science competition. At this point the reader may guess that the evil Dr Foster is going to rig the competition.

(Silly aside: yes, the acronym reads CCCP. That was an honest accident and not engineered by some communist plot. People born after 1989 may not get it.)

This is the very basic structure for a blurb. From this basic blurb, I would put the book in Urban Fantasy as it's set in a contemporary world, unless the blurb says that the whole book is set in a fantasy land, or the university teaches magic, in which case I would probably put it in Epic Fantasy, or Comedic Fantasy, if it's meant to be funny. Use your judgement.

In the case of Urban Fantasy, I would put a dark cover on it if the book included dark elements (murder, serious threats to life and dark magic) or a cartoonish cover if it was for younger readers or if the book was funny.

If Epic Fantasy, I would get an artist to draw a cover with orcs and elves and a stately building and I would get the artist to use dark colours if the tone of the book was dark and lighter colours if the book was funny. I would use a different artist for a dark book than I would for a funny book.

This, then, is how the complete presentation package comes together. The title, cover and blurb reflect what's inside. They all point in the same direction so that your potential reader can get a good feel for what type of book it is.

But before we continue, there are a few other important things . . .

The Ugly Stepchild

…OF SELF-PUBLISHING is formatting.

For those who say formatting doesn't matter, a single look at a poorly formatted book is enough to dispel this notion.

Try reading a book that hits you in the face with a "wall of text" because of paragraphs that are too large and too densely spaced, or where paragraphs don't have indents (fiction) or an empty line between them (non-fiction) to space them out. Or where the indents are strangely wide, or the chapters mushed together, or . . . the list is endless.

People click away from books because the text looks "wrong", even if they can't formulate what "wrong" is.

Formatting is not hard. You can do it yourself. At the very basic level, formatting uses HTML code. An ebook is a web document.

There are guides for formatting your own books, for example, Guido Henkel's *Zen of eBook Formatting*.

Simple, right?

Er, no. For starters, there are two formats: MOBI for Amazon books and EPUB for the rest. Amazon has a guide up for how to produce MOBI files, and you'll have to do something different for your EPUB files.

EPUB is a notoriously finicky and unstable format. It doesn't always validate and is a little bit different for each device. You will need to know about the EPUB2 and EPUB3 standards and all the issues relating to display on different devices and also what different stores allow.

Fortunately, for the very beginners, most sales platforms allow you to upload DOC files. Amazon does this, Kobo does this, and the aggregators Draft 2 Digital and Smashwords do this, but at Smashwords you will have to download the *Smashwords Style Guide* and follow it to the letter. As is, this guide is an excellent primer for those who don't know anything about book formatting conventions, and even if you only plan on formatting your own print books, I strongly recommend that you get it. It's free.

Although you can upload Word files and let the retailer sites convert them for you, their formatting output is really basic and sometimes errors creep in, especially if your Word file is messy and contains a lot of invisible character format codes. In this case, you may need to nuke the file as described in the Smashwords Style Guide. Really, get it, even if you never plan to do your own formatting. It is such an excellent explanation of how text editors work in general.

Using the above options, you can, relatively successfully, format a basic text.

But what if you want to add formatting elements such as flourishes with chapter headings, and different fonts for specific purposes? For example if you have an AI speak, you may want to put those lines in monospace Courier font. Or if you write non-fiction, you may want to add bullet points or tables. And any book needs a nice title page, of course, because this highly enhances the free sample that people are going to see on retailer sites.

Then the requirement that an ebook has a Table of Contents . . . Amazon has made this a requirement for files sold on their website. It may seem a bit silly to you to include a Table of Contents in a fiction book, but try flipping through an ebook to find a certain scene and you'll get why this is a requirement.

Formatting emergencies have a habit of sneaking up on you. Readers will not hesitate to let you know about problems you were not aware of, and of course when something like this crops up, it needs to be fixed yesterday.

You may not know how to fix it or where the problem lies. You may need to call in someone who makes formatting their specialty.

In short, there are a number of formatting options:

   ♦   DIY, with your own coding. Time-intensive, and it takes a bit of research and knowledge to make files that look pretty. Use Guido Henkel's guide.

♦ You can upload DOC files to various sites, and some of those sites will allow you to use the files they generate elsewhere. This requires a clean DOC file and you may need to manually produce your own Table of Contents. The Smashwords Style Guide is good for this.

♦ You can buy or download software that generates ebook files. Some of the options are fairly basic, but others are sophisticated. If you have a Mac, I absolutely recommend that you buy a piece of software called Vellum, which you can also use to format your print books. An unlimited licence costs $250 at the time of writing, but it formats your files in minutes, the files look extremely nice, are optimised for each sales platform and each device and the Vellum people are extremely on the ball about changes in requirements. This and a program called Scrivener, and the fact that you need a Mac to upload files directly to Apple, is the reason that most serious writers own a Mac.

♦ For the PC, there is a free program called Sigil and another program called Jutoh. It is about $40.

♦ Or you can pay someone to do it for you at $25-100 per file. This can be a fairly basic service, but if you're going to spend money, I recommend spending it on someone who delivers nice, professional-looking work that's indistinguishable from or even better than the ebooks from major publishers.

However you choose to do it is up to you and will depend on the amount of money and time you have.

But don't make the mistake of treating formatting like the ugly stepchild. It is important.

In late 2014, I was doing my own formatting through the EPUB generation capability in InDesign. I sold a lot of books on Kobo and after I made a change, I was made aware that those files were flawed in some cases.

When I did some computer science subjects at university, the lecturer would always start his large plenary lectures off with the saying "To err is human, but to completely f* things up requires a computer." A programming malfunction, even a small one, usually renders a file unusable. In my case, it put each word on a separate page. Urgh!

It was just before Christmas and I had zero time to sort it out. I ran around like the proverbial chook without a head and hired two formatters. One of them I still use today (hi, Rick!) because his work is very pretty and it helped me, barely a month later, secure my first Bookbub.

Get this: Bookbub had rejected this title about eight times. I reformatted the book with a nice title page and nice chapter headings and they accepted me.

Formatting is important. Take it from me.

An emergency formatting hack

If ever you have a formatting emergency, or you need to format a file for Advanced Reader Copies or similar reason, go to
Draft2Digital and open an account if you don't already have
one (and you should. They're really cool for reasons I'll tell
you about later). It's free. Upload your DOC file as new book,
then follow the publishing process until you get to the screen
where you can download sample EPUB and MOBI files. Do
this. Use those files to upload to retailers or send to your readers. It costs nothing, and D2D absolutely allows you to do this.

Don't Forget The Back Matter

ONE OF THE MOST important elements in setting up your book for sale is quite simple. It's the book's back matter.

These are the About the Author and Also By sections in the back of your book, where you list your contacts, your website and other books you have written.

In the back matter, you get to tell people what to do next.

Make no mistake, people are lazy and love being told what to do.

Do you want them to review the book? Tell them. Do you want them to sign up for your mailing list? Tell them. Do you want them to buy the next book? Tell them. Make a page for each of these things on your website and put links in the book's back matter.

You may ask: is it not better to link directly to the next book on the retailer site? It can be, depending on your aim and you may like to try this.

My aim in the three-year plan is to take control of as much of my audience as I can get. I want as many people as possible on my mailing list, and I want them away from the retailer sites. Of course I will send them back to those sites so that they can buy the book, but I prefer to know who they are first. At the very least I want to know where they came from and how many of them clicked the link.

Also, if you include links to retailer sites, you will have to compile a different ebook file for each retailer, because they will not let you upload a file with a competitor's links in the back. Fancy that.

So, where do you put these links?

The most important piece of real estate in your back matter is immediately following the end of the book, and before the page header for the About The Author section. So you'll finish the text, and there will be a scene break character, usually asterisks, and your closing message will come after that. In my case, it reads something like:

Thank you for reading [book]. In the next book of the series [add a brief tidbit about the next book]. Get [title of the next book] here.

The last sentence would be a live link to a page on my website.

One of the very important things I can do on this page is let the reader know when the next book will be out, if it isn't out yet, and add a signup page to be notified.

But what if you like to link to a retailer page, and you don't have it yet because the book hasn't been published? In that case, use an editable link redirect service like SmartURL or the WordPress plug-in prettylinks. Point the link at the page on your website, and insert the shortcode in your book. Then swap over the link to point to the retailer site later. Now you don't need to edit your ebook in order to change the link.

Amazon has the very annoying habit of inserting its own recommendation page immediately after the end of the book. If you are exclusive to Amazon, you may not mind this, but if you want people to visit a website, you will need to be vigilant about this. Simply re-uploading the book file will take care of this.

Here is another important thing: When you have a mailing list signup link in your books, make sure you put it in the front as well as the back.

I know it sounds silly. Why ask people to sign up before they've even read the book?

Consider someone who is as anal as I am: when I finish reading a book, I go back to the first page and close the book, so that it won't continue to show as "reading now" on my e-reader.

Say I read a book, and two days later I was still thinking about it and wanted to sign up for when the next book comes out. If I closed the book, I would have to wade through the entire book to get to the signup link at the end.

Even if you're not as anal as I am, and don't get why, put the link in the front of the book anyway. We'll come back to this issue a few times in this book.

You Are Now Ready To Sell Your Book

THERE YOU GO!

You are now ready to start selling your books. They're packaged nicely, look great, you have done your best to make sure your catalogue is of the best quality you can put out.

You have added the appropriate links where they need to be.

Now we can deal with the things you need to do to set up your sales strategies.

Let's start selling this puppy.

The Seriously Boring Crap That's Really Important

FIRST I'M GOING to talk to you about accounting. I know, I know, I can hardly think of a more yawn-inducing subject on the planet. Sadly, it's also really important. A wrong decision can cost you a lot of money and involve a lot of work to put right.

Before you start selling, you need the following:

A bank account dedicated to your sales income.

A tax ID for the same

If you're envisaging setting up as a commercial writer, you're a business—and if you weren't, you probably wouldn't be reading this book—and you should set up a business for your books. How you do this depends on where you live. Consult a local accountant. In general these options probably exist: you can set up as a sole trader or as publishing business. A publishing business is likely to be the more expensive of the two options, but does offer you the opportunity to publish other people's work, and in most countries has the most rigorous protection of your personal assets in case of a claim.

You might be able to set up as a sole trader or equivalent and this would cover just you, with fewer administrative hoops.

Why you should do this: setting up as a business allows you to claim expenses as tax deductions. These expenses can be quite considerable, especially in the beginning: editing, cover design, formatting, ads, the cost of setting up a website. If you're going to start spending this sort of money, it's silly not to set up a business and claim those costs as deductions, because they are costs incurred in producing your income.

Retailers are by law required to withhold tax.

All retailers—listed in the next chapter—will ask you for a tax ID. Give them your business bank account and your business tax ID. At the end of the year, the retailer will send you a statement with how much tax they withheld on your behalf, and you can use this in your annual tax return to claim deductions.

Some of them will also ask you for a US tax ID, even if you're not in the US. These retailers will withhold 30% of your earnings if you don't supply this. They will include this in your statement and you are likely to be able to claim it against local tax, but this requires a clued-up accountant.

Better to bite the bullet and get the US tax ID.

An EIN (Employer Identification Number) for non-US sellers is easily obtained over the phone, especially if you download the form, fill it out according to the instructions, and read out your replies to the operator. You need this form. The number is on the form.

Tip for the typically phone-phobic writer: set up Skype on your phone, drop a few dollars into the account and use that. Don't worry that they'll put you on hold—they will. I put $20 into my account when setting this up, rang the US tax office from Australia, was put on hold for 45 minutes—terrible hold music! I still have $15 of that money, even though I've been ringing relatives in Europe for an hour every month since then.

An important point to consider if you have a paying day job: many jobs, especially in higher management, higher education, manufacturing, technology or research, include non-compete clauses in their contracts.

While it is true that a full-time employer can't dictate what you do in your spare time, they have a lot more leverage if you make money from your spare time activity, or if they perceive this activity as competing with your contract of employment. There are also issues surrounding confidentiality, ownership of work or knowledge and income derived from your employment with them.

If you work in a medical research lab and write historical romance, your employer is unlikely to have an issue with it. However, if you wrote medical thrillers, they just might. Especially if your book suddenly took off.

Therefore, dust off that contract and see what it says about other income. You may, as I was, be unpleasantly surprised.

To-do list:

- Set up a company or sole trader

- Get a tax ID for this entity

- Get US EIN for this entity

- Get a bank account for this entity

- Check the contract of employment for your day job for nasty clauses about income or proprietary knowledge

Where To Sell

CURRENTLY, THERE ARE five major retailers and three major aggregators—sites that distribute your book to retailer sites on your behalf. Most will pay you 60-70% of your book's retail price. I will go through the options here, and list major features of each, but there is much I don't cover. I strongly suggest that you visit the links given here and read the terms and conditions yourself.

Also, things change very quickly, and it's likely that this page will be out-of-date the day after I finished typing it.

Amazon Kindle Direct Publishing

You simply have to be here. This is the largest ebook retailer. Features separate retail sites in the US, the UK, Canada, Mexico, Brazil, Germany, France, Spain, Italy, Japan and Australia. You get 70% of royalties for most books priced between $2.99

and $9.99 and 35% outside that range. Payment is through cheque or bank account in some countries, or EFT in the US. Outside the US they use "wire transfer" rather than IFT, which can mean a substantial extra banking cost for you if you're not in the US or UK. Otherwise, select the cheque option. If cheque costs are onerous, email them to stop payment and release it once every six months. That way you're not traipsing to the bank every month and subsidising the manager's BMW.

If you're not in the US, they will accept your local tax ID if you're in a country that has a tax treaty with the US.

Amazon's help function is outsourced to some cheap country and gives you copy-and-pasted replies, which is unhelpful when you have a real problem. They're also not always correct.

They can also be draconian, and they ban before they warn.

Kobo Writing Life

The Kobo Writing Life portal is one of the prettiest and easiest to use. Who can resist that awesome map that tells you where in the world you have sold?

Payment: 70% of royalties for prices over $2.99. Note: no upper price cap.

Kobo's main office resides in Canada, and this alone makes it a much more international seller than Amazon. They also sell only books, and only ebooks at that. They sell their own devices and have a free app that everyone can use. They do not require an EIN, and your local tax ID will do just fine.

Your dashboard features a promotions tab which allows you to apply to take part in store-run promotions, most of which won't involve any up-front costs.

Their help function is run by real humans and you can strike a good one, or wait days for a reply. One of the known issues of the accounts is that it's sometimes hard to set up payment. Payment is through Western Union into your bank account, but sometimes it takes a bit of help from their side to set up the bank account correctly.

Barnes and Noble

Accessed through NOOK Press. You need to be in the US to set up an account. Since I am not, I cannot sell there, but various people have told me that the site is buggy and you might as well use an aggregator for all the frustration it causes. Their words, not mine.

One of the most ridiculous things about Nook is that they don't work on weekends. Apparently, changes to your book (and pricing) require a human hamster to run on a wheel, and the site is frozen on the weekend.

Apple

You have to own a Mac in order to run the upload software iTunes Producer. If you don't have one, you can use a service called Mac In Cloud to access it. If you're used to the Apple OS, then you'll find it relatively easy. If have never used a Mac then You. Cannot. Find. Anything. Be prepared for some frustration. Their help function is reasonably good.

They do require an EIN.

Think clearly how you're going to set up your account structure before you apply. DON'T use your personal AppleID to create your account, because it will take all your details from there. You cannot change this. Create an AppleID specifically for your business and attach all the appropriate business-related accounts, credit cards and tax IDs to it.

Google Play

If you click on the link, you may find a page that says they're not accepting new accounts. You may also be lucky and strike the very short periods of time that Google Play is open for the registration of new accounts.

If you can't open an account, the Google Play store is accessible through some aggregators, most importantly StreetLib and Pronoun.

On Google Play itself, you get 52% of recommended retail price. They have the tendency to discount, usually by about 30%, without your approval. This can both be annoying and a boon. If they discount, you still get 52% of the price you have set, so if you jack up the price, you will end up getting a lot more per book than on the other retailers.

Google Play does not require an EIN, and pays into your bank account without silly hoops or fees.

The site is a bit onerous, but believe me, it used to be a lot worse, and these days it's reasonably easy to understand, and changes to your books and pricing are lightning fast.

Smashwords

In addition to being an aggregator, Smashwords also has their own store. They distribute to all major retailers except Amazon and Google Play, and a lot of smaller places, including library suppliers. The website looks very 1990's, and a lot of smut with insanely bad covers gets sold there. But some people in some countries swear by Smashwords. The nifty thing about Smashwords is their coupons. These allow you to make a book free—and email the codes to the members of your ARC team.

They pay monthly (if someone tells you that they pay quarterly, that is what they used to do until recently), use PayPal or cheque but with a strong preference for PayPal, and take 10% of your earnings.

They do require an EIN.

Draft 2 Digital

Aggregator only, although they are starting to do some really interesting things, like offering audio books. They've also recently introduced formatting templates for ebooks.

Distributes to major retailers except Amazon and Google Play. The website is nice and sleek and easy to use. They host nifty universal links, where you can generate just one link for your book to use in advertising, taking the reader to their retailer of choice in their country. Beware, though, that those links don't always work, especially for readers who are not in the US. They pay through bank transfer or PayPal or and require an EIN.

Pronoun

The new kid on the block at the time of writing this book. There are a number of advantages of going with them:

♦ They are the only aggregator that will upload to Amazon

♦ You will get the full 70% of sales in the US; Pronoun takes no cut

♦ Outside the US you get 41%. For me personally, this is the killer. I sell a lot more outside the US than in.

♦ You can get preorders for longer than 3 months on Amazon

♦ Pays 70% of sales on books under $2.99 and over $9.99 on Amazon

♦ They give a lot of data

Disadvantages: suspicious as we all are, everyone is wondering where the catch is. They're owned by Pan Macmillan, and maybe they're using the data to gain insight into what self-publishers are doing. It's a mystery.

Smaller retail sites

Drivethrufiction, good especially for science fiction and fantasy.

Smaller aggregator sites

Streetlib (recommended, can get you into Google Play), XinXii (not recommended, impossible to update and remove books) and the up-and-coming PublishDrive.

Should you use an aggregator or go direct?

I believe that you should always go direct to sites that give you special promotional opportunities that would not be available otherwise, most notably Amazon and Kobo. Otherwise, it's up to you.

Pros of using an aggregator:

♦   Less work

♦   One account to manage

♦   One payment

Cons of using an aggregator:

♦   10% may not sound like much, and it isn't when you earn $60 per month. But it becomes a lot more when you earn $600 per month. When you earn $6000 per month, you can pay an accountant with the money you save.

♦   You may not be eligible for promotions on retailer websites, notably Kobo

Think carefully, because when you go with an aggregator and then go direct, you may lose all your reviews for that book. Since people are more likely to review on other sites that are not Amazon, losing 900 reviews on Kobo just because you got sick of paying an aggregator $100 of your earnings per month is a difficult decision. If you intend to move your books across, it pays to email the retailers, because they may be able to migrate your reviews over for you.

Free book delivery services

If you want to give your books away and collect email addresses, you may want to get an account at Bookfunnel and Instafreebie. There will be much more about these in *Mailing Lists Unboxed*, because these services integrate really well with your mailing list.

Despite the fact that they both offer this service, they are not the same.

Instafreebie comes with a built-in promotion engine that will put your free book in the hands of people you didn't know.

Bookfunnel concentrates on getting the book onto people's devices with the most ease possible. You will realise that this is an important function once you give your book for free to list subscribers and start getting "How do I get this on my Kindle?" emails.

To-do list:

◆   Get a KDP account

◆   Decide how much effort you want to invest into putting your books up at retailers, and decide if you want to go with an aggregator or list direct.

◆   Get accounts on other retailers

◆   Start uploading your books!

Presentation

MOST SITES WILL give you a few—not many but a few—tools to enhance the presentation of your book on their site.

You will upload your standard blurb and cover to each site, but there are some aspects where the sites differ, notably in the categories and searchability of books.

Amazon

The most important thing you need to do is make sure you claim your Author Central page. You can do this from your KDP dashboard, or by googling Author Central. If you are registered with Author Central, you can make an author profile page that includes a bio, has an RSS link to your blog or Twitter account, contains images or a video and includes all your books. It's little known that you need to do this separately for Amazon US, UK, Germany and France. Those are the only Amazon stores that have Author Central profiles.

Next you have to make sure that Amazon produces a series page for your series. You do this by entering the exact same series name in the appropriate box when you upload your book. If Amazon doesn't create the page automatically, email them.

Categories: Amazon has put out helpful information about how to get your book into specialised categories using specific keywords. You can find it here.

Kobo

Kobo has a nice series feature that allows you to add all kinds of books to your series, because they don't require books to be numbered. Kobo allows three categories.

The most important part about the Kobo dashboard is that you should make sure that you get the "Promotions" tab. You will find this right underneath the page header. If you can't see it, email and ask. The feature is in beta and they will evaluate each request on merit. If you have only one book or your covers look very homemade, they are unlikely to accept. But you got this far into the book—you know you need nice covers, right?

IBooks

If you list on iBooks directly, you will be faced with a staggering number of possible categories in many different library classification systems in the world. I'm not sure how much it adds to fill out all of them, but I'd fill out those for the countries where you hope to sell. Apple also has a unique system of pricing where you can easily gauge whether your price is high or low for books in that country.

To-do list:

♦   Visit book pages in your genre on all retailers

♦   Look for features that allow your books to stand out that are specific to the retailer

♦   Use them

Exclusive Or Wide?

AS EVIDENCE TO the divisive power wielded by Amazon, there is a subscription program called Kindle Unlimited (KU) or KDP Select that will place your book in a library where it can be "borrowed" by readers for a flat fee of $10 per month.

On the side of the writers and publishers, it requires your book to be exclusive to Amazon. It also cannot be part of a collection that is available anywhere else—whether on Amazon, and even in KU or not.

Should you enter this program?

Before I'll say anything else, I'll say that this is 100% typically Amazon to instate something as ridiculously divisive as this. They want self-published authors to list on this service. The traditional publishers are mostly running a mile from it, probably because of the relatively low compensation, about 0.4 of a cent per page read. Since traditionally published books usually have much higher prices, it makes zero sense for them to list in the program. If they are in the program, they often have the exclusivity requirement waived.

Much as I personally detest the program, or rather its exclusivity requirement, I advise you to think about it and consider it carefully.

It might be advantageous if:

♦   You are a very new writer and feel overwhelmed with the thought of creating accounts and uploading files at several retailers.

♦   You expect your biggest audience to be in the US.

♦   You like a set-and-forget approach for the time being

♦   You are trying out different audiences.

Participation in the program is only for three months at a time, and during this period your book cannot be available anywhere on the Internet other than Amazon, including your own website. I would advocate that if you are considering it, you only enter the program with "virgin" books, ones that haven't been uploaded anywhere yet. Some of the retailers upload your books to resellers or partner sites, and it's often near-impossible to have them taken down.

Here are some of my objections against the program.

♦   Yes, it is true that books in Kindle Unlimited are often ranked higher in the Amazon US store than those that are not, but how much of that is artificial? Ranking jumps when someone borrows a book, but you only get paid once someone reads the book, and that may not happen at all, leaving you with the false impression that ranking equates money, while foregoing real money you could have made elsewhere.

♦ While you are in the program, you're not building your audience elsewhere. This affects your long-term sustainability of sales. Note that this book is about building long-term sustainability.

♦ If you're interested in international sales, don't enter the program. When I have a stand at local cons in Australia, and I tell people that my books are also available as ebooks, the only thing I'm ever asked is if they're on iBooks.

♦ Certain genres are dominated by Kindle Unlimited books, does that mean you should be in it, too? Well, how about readers of that genre who browse on non-Amazon stores? They're presented with a diminished choice and are more likely to buy your book if it's well-presented. A crowded genre in KU means a less competitive genre on other stores.

♦ Amazon can—and does—occasionally pull out the rug from under everyone by making changes to the program or the payment structure. This happened in July 2015, and some authors saw their incomes slashed by 90%. Better play it safe and don't have all your books in the program so that you can get by with income from outside, if necessary. There is no worse time to start building an audience on non-Amazon stores than when everybody else is scrambling to do the same. Start building your audience and put your books wide before the next KU-poca-lypse sends in the droves of desperate.

♦ Not only that, but Amazon cannot actually reliably record the number of pages read. You'll often get reports of people reading one page. Do you know what happens? A reader finishes a book and flips back to the front cover before reconnecting the Kin-dle to the wifi. And you get paid for only one page instead of 400.

♦ Amazon also plays around with what constitutes a page. As you know, a page in a digital book is an ex-tremely arbitrary concept. Amazon can decide—and has done things like this—that instead of 250 words, a page is now 260 words, and screw everyone over in the process. Amazon excels at screwing people over like this. Of course, they never, ever communi-cate with their content providers either, so if you try to fiddle with page length through certain methods you've learned about at forums, next thing you know you'll get an email that your account is suspended. Don't shake your head, I've seen this happen often enough.

♦ The structure of the program—one that divorces reader payments from payment to authors—lends itself perfectly to scamming. The following still hap-pens frequently:

A scammer produces a book full of rubbish, such as a copied book hauled twice through Google Trans-late so that it no longer trips the plagiarism filters, and then sticks a number of these "books" together so that they make up 3000 "pages", the maximum number of pages allowable for a book in Kindle Unlimited. They then engage clickfarms with Kindle Unlimited subscriptions to borrow and flip through these books so that they get paid for the page reads. It's an entirely closed system that does not rely on readers, but it propels junk books to the top of the charts where they take up spaces, and the "authors" get paid money and bonuses that should be paid to legitimate authors. Amazon does little to stop it.

Do you really want to mix with that nonsense?

Well, make your decision, and run with the consequences. Some people do really well in the program, and I only suggest that you consider it.

The only thing you should absolutely avoid is to flip-flop between being exclusive and wide. There is no better way to annoy your readers. People in Kindle Unlimited are a different audience. You should see it as a separate store, but one that requires you to exclude all others. People with a subscription are likely to be in the US, read a lot, and are concentrated in Romance. They do buy books, but many prefer to read them as part of their subscription.

People who are on the other stores are generally happy to pay a bit more than people on Amazon, they are more likely to be outside the US, and they don't read quite as much.

Before you say that it's obviously better to go where voracious readers are, it may be that those voracious readers don't happen to be in your genre. And that your work may not appeal as much to US audiences as international audiences.

My point is, the audiences who read in KU and those who

don't are not the same people.

Each time you pull your books from other stores and go into KU, or vice versa, you start over with another audience and annoy the readers you already had. Make up your mind and stay there.

To-do list:

♦   Consider who your audience is likely to be, where they are likely to be, and decide if you want to be exclusive or not

First Free Or 99¢?

AS YOU WILL have noticed in the brief outline of the three-year plan, I told you to make book 1 of each series free.

Lately, there has been a bit of backlash against free books from within the writing community, because "There are too many free books," and "The permafree is dead."

What they mean to say is that, unlike a fairly brief honeymoon period when people were going on free book binges, getting readers to download the free book has become work. You have to lead the readers to the free book. They won't discover it by themselves.

Yes, there are a lot of free books, and yes, having a free book still works, if you use it correctly.

NOT using it correctly means making the book free and sitting back waiting for the hordes to come.

Using it correctly means telling people, "Here is book 1 in my series free," and leading them to where they can download the book.

Many, many companies use the tactic of the free sample. They have done this since the beginning of commerce and I suspect they will continue to do this until the end of the world, possibly even after.

Giving away free content in order to entice people to buy the rest works:

♦   If your content is good.

♦   If you make sure that people see that content.

Say I ran a butchery that had just won an award for sausages, and I created an offer that said "Get 10 sausages free with a kilo of steak!"

I printed the offer on flyers showing nice juicy sausages and I wanted as many people as possible to see it.

Would I:

♦   Put the leaflets in a stack on a table in front of the post office in the shopping centre?

♦   Pay the next-door neighbour's teenage daughter to put 500 flyers in letterboxes around the suburb?

♦   Pay the teenage daughter and her friend to come to the shopping centre on a busy Saturday morning, give them sausage-themed shirts and put them inside the entrance of the shopping centre with a barbecue with sizzling sausage pieces people could try and vouchers for free sausages with your steak right there at your shop which happens to be just inside the entrance as well?

Each of these options would cost increasingly more, but I bet the more people can try, the more they will buy.

(Excuse me, now I feel like eating sausages.)

Free works if you put in the effort to make it work. You make your book free, and then you run ads. These could be ad sites, or Facebook or AMS (Amazon Marketing Services—via your KDP dashboard) or cross-promotions. Point is: you need to advertise your free book.

But the above example is also exactly why I no longer have my free books on retailer sites. Most of these sites don't like the top spots in their genre rankings to be cluttered with free books. They want the George R.R. Martins and J.K. Rowlings to occupy those spots. They have reduced the visibility of free books and sometimes even cheap books, and made it much harder for people to find them. Therefore you, the author, drive the traffic to these books. Therefore, also, you can drive the traffic to where you want these people to download the free book. In my case, I want people to go to a place where they need to leave their email address in order to get the free book.

So what, then, if you no longer have the books free on the retailer sites, should you price the books? Some people say 99¢, but I've put all mine up to $3.99. Why?

Because, similar to free, 99¢ only gets attention if you run a sale. Therefore if you're not running a sale, put the price up so that you have somewhere to move down to if you do want to have a sale.

But won't those people get annoyed if they buy the book and then find out they could have gotten it for free?

You remember how I said to put your signup link in the front of the book? It will probably say something like "Get this book for free if you sign up for my mailing list." It will show up in Amazon's "Look Inside" and the link will be live. You thought you couldn't enter live links in your author profile or your book pages on Amazon? Yes, you can.

People who are sensitive to the "Could have gotten this for free" issue will see it and will sign up. Problem solved.

The most important thing to take away from the free vs. paid debate is that free is a tool. Amazon, Kobo, iBooks etc. are mere delivery methods. When considering whether your book should be free or not, this should go hand in hand with your consideration of how you're going to use the tool and what methods you will use to get the free books into the hands of potential readers. Just "make it free" by itself is not a method.

My books are still free. Readers can get them by signing up for my mailing list. I use platforms other than the retailers (Bookfunnel and Instafreebie) to deliver the free books. At this point in time, those are my methods, but they will likely change in the future.

The blindingly non-obvious issue for the new writer

How do you make a book permanently free on Amazon? Because the upload menu won't allow you to do it, yet you can see the free books on the site. How on Earth did the writers do that?

First, you upload your book to other retailers, and make it free there. If your book sells reasonably well, Amazon is likely to make the book free on its own. It's quite sensitive to prices on iBooks and Google Play in particular.

If your book doesn't sell so well, an email may be called for. Grab the links to your free book on the other retailers (don't forget the links in other countries), and email KDP support with those links, using the link in your dashboard. Ask them to make it free, because the book is free on Apple and Kobo and Nook, and look, here are the links if you guys want to check it.

Once you've sent the email with the links to the free book in the US, UK, Canada, Australia and wherever else Amazon has stores and you want it free, they will send you back a snarky canned reply that "free is at their discretion" or some rubbish like that. But they will make it free anyway. In the few very limited cases where it doesn't happen, email again. You're highly unlikely to hit the same grumpy customer rep. If you want to make it free because, say, you snagged a free Bookbub, send this email not too long before the ad. I advocate two weeks. Amazon will make your book free in all nominated territories, but mainland Europe has funny laws about free and low pricing and won't keep the books free in Germany. Germany is a fairly sizeable proportion of my market, so that's something to consider.

To-do list:

♦ Decide what your sales strategy is going to look like. Will you use retailers as the delivery mechanism for your free books, or will you collect the email addresses of people who download your free books?

♦ Decide how you are going to advertise your free books

What About Print?

MANY WRITERS DREAM of seeing their books on the shelves in their favourite bookstore. There is something romantic about paper books that can't be replaced by ebooks.

But this area is all stitched up by the publishing industry. They have the investment-heavy channels that supply the books, the reps that travel around to the bookshops that sell the books to the owners, and the back-end system setup that bookshops use, with a scan of the ISBN, to order or re-order their stock.

They also give the bookshops the discounts they need in order to make a profit and pay the rent or mortgage, and pay their staff. And oh, themselves.

Bing-bing-bing! Bookstores need to make money in order to survive. They don't do it for love of books (although many of course also do), they don't do it so that we can feel comforted to know that old bookshops still exist, they do it because they have to pay their bills.

There is a huge industry that lies behind the books that you see for sale on the shelves and it is also one where it is very hard to compete without the bulk discounts and onerous returns policies that make selling your Print On Demand books a lot of work for not much money.

I'm not entirely saying don't do it, because there are some cases where you might want to give it a go, but it's very hard to make decent money selling print books.

If you write non-fiction, especially non-fiction that is tied to your locality, if you're a local author and are well-known locally or if you write picture-heavy non-fiction, you will find that your sales will naturally skew towards print anyway and you may try.

But it's hard and a lot of work.

In 2000, I published a full colour non-fiction book. I had it printed in Hong Kong, shipped to Australia, and I paid the customs duties. I sent flyers to about 800 bookshops and visited whichever ones I could reach while also having young children. It was a lot of work, but because I knew the—very specialised—market, I sold a lot of books. Would I do it again today? Nup. I'd probably make a pay-for-content website. For one, do you realise how heavy books are?

For fiction authors, especially of adult fiction, print is far less than 5% of our sales. If you rocked up to a bookshop, managed to be there at the time the book buyer was in, held the book under her nose, why would you think she would even consider you? She probably gets asked the same question by at least 2-3 suckers published by vanity presses per week. She's probably been burned a few times.

You can add print to your available formats, but do so only if you can do it easily or cheaply.

If you can format your own books, if you have InDesign and know a bit about print formatting, sure, why not, but if you have to pay someone to format it, I would think twice, or I'd at least wait until I was selling quite well.

If you do want to go the print route, there are two companies to consider.

CreateSpace is by far the easiest to deal with. They're owned by Amazon, will automatically upload your books to Amazon and link them with your ebooks. Uploading books there is free. They can also supply you with an ISBN for free, and distribute your book to other booksellers. They pay by cheque (and direct deposit if you're in the US) and need an EIN.

IngramSpark are a little bit more upmarket, more robust. They are not free (although they do have periods when setting up new books is free). They also charge if you have to make changes. They require an ISBN; they can do hardcovers and distribute your book to retailers. The rumour goes that bookshops and libraries are more likely to order through them. My counterargument is that, since your print sales are likely to be so small, will the cost of setting up through them outweigh the potential for increased sales?

For both companies, you'll need a print-ready PDF. Done properly, this is not an easy document to create. If you really want to do this in a nice way, you should probably hire someone who knows about placement, about rivers and valleys, about kerning and headers and footers, master templates and whatnot.

CreateSpace has handy templates that you can download. They used to allow you to upload Word files, but as of recently, they don't seem to allow that anymore. The world of Print On Demand self-publishing is in a status of flux, with KDP having introduced KDP print, where you can upload your print book directly via the KDP ebook publishing platform, also in print-ready PDF only. Yes, Amazon already owns CreateSpace. No, no one understands why they're creating direct competition with their own company. As I said, it's in a state of flux and what I say here will probably be out of date next month.

Professionals make print-ready PDFs with InDesign, which is not easy to learn and not cheap. You can also make a reasonably nice file with Vellum. Draft2Digital also produces PDFs, but I haven't seen their quality.

It is highly likely that both the Vellum and D2D options are of "this'll do" quality. Print book formatting to professional standards absolutely requires a real human. It's also a dubious investment if you have to pay for it, because print sales are unlikely to be a major source of income.

But as an aside, tell me: when did you last visit your favourite bookstore? Did you go down there to find that they didn't stock what you wanted, or did you even find it all boarded up?

Did you go home and order the book you wanted online instead?

Much as the notion of quaint old bookstores is romantic, it also isn't terribly practical for either reader or owner—for readers, because bookstores seem to carry an ever-shrinking range of books; for owners, because carrying even that reduced number of titles can't make you a profit. People order everything online. Think about it: online, you can find what you want, order it, and it's delivered to your door. See this Author Earnings report for some startling stats on book sales.

So what do you do when you own a bookstore? You start selling gifts, because people still buy books as gifts. You start selling pretty books and fashionable books that are sure to give you a return.

Sad as it is, this appears to be the way things are going. People don't have so much time for shopping and browsing. Mostly, people have heard recommendations from friends and want that particular book. They don't need recommendations from the bookshop owner anymore.

To-do list:

♦   Decide if and when you want print books, and why

♦   Decide on a formatting process or service

♦   Open an account at CreateSpace or IngramSpark

♦   Upload your book

♦   Make sure it gets linked with your ebook on Amazon (you may need to email KDP if this doesn't happen within a few days)

Does Your Book Need An ISBN?

THE QUESTION OF ISBNS in self-publishing comes up a bit. Does your book need one?

If you live in the wonderful countries of New Zealand or Canada, you can skip this section. ISBNs are free, so go be merry, ask for a bunch of them and stick them on all your books.

For the rest of us poor sods who have to pay and then register the damn things with some daft agency . . .

Traditionalists are adamant that an ISBN is "essential" and that it makes you look "professional".

I have to admit to being a bit allergic to that latter word: "professional". It's a word that's making a beeline for my list of hated words, because in the writer space, it's so often used to put down "people who disagree with me".

In the 1990's in the heydays of my non-fiction bookselling, I dealt with a publishing company in Germany. They had about 40-odd books out and made a living from this. None of their books had ISBNs. To me, it was a small pain in the butt, because I listed their books on websites that liked to get ISBNs and not having them put their books in the dungeon of the pre-1960s books that did not have ISBNs. Bookshops need IS-BNs to enter books in their system, and so do libraries. Despite failing the traditional industry, the German publisher's books sold quite well. They were books on diving and sea life and I suspect many were sold through specialist retailers, like dive shops. This was in the publisher-controlled, pre-ebook time.

Back then, I published some books and bought ISBNs for them, because bookshops needed them. I even bought a block of ISBNs for my first lot of ebooks. But after I did that, I found it impossible to register them through the Thorpe-Bowker website. They gave me no help and didn't reply to my emails, so I gave up and had a rethink: what do you actually pay for when you buy ISBNs?

Amazon doesn't require one.

If you make a print version through CreateSpace, they will give you a free ISBN to satisfy bookshop systems. Authors of popular books report that the CreateSpace ISBN does not deter bookshops from ordering. Anyway, bookshops are not your focus. If they are, seek a traditional publisher.

None of the other retailers require ISBNs. In fact, one of the Author Earning reports looked at the ISBN situation for the top 120,000 books at Amazon. A whopping thirty percent do not have ISBNs. Earnings and sales do not suffer. In fact, the report shows higher sales and income for books without IS-BNs. Now before we all draw conclusions from that, let's just say that sales do not suffer.

Think about it: self-publishers say (and this has been proven right) that the vast majority of buyers do not care who published a book. Certainly buyers can rarely name the publisher of books they buy. Why then should they care about whether or not it has an ISBN?

"Oh, but it looks PROFESSIONAL!"

Seriously, bollocks. All an ISBN does is line the pockets of an industry that, by self-publishing, we have already chosen to step away from.

Sure, buy an ISBN if you want, but unless your focus is print and bookshops and libraries, it's money wasted.

In the words of Author Earnings:

"What we can say for sure is that the clear lack of any material benefit in the marketplace makes the cost of purchasing an ISBN for an ebook very difficult to justify—the same money would be far better invested instead in better professional editing, proofreading, formatting, cover art, and the like."

To-do list:

♦ If you want ISBNs, get them now. Buy them in a block owned by your company, don't go into one of those share-buy schemes.

Other Formats

WHERE ELSE DOES IT make sense to make your book available?

Audio

Audio books are becoming very popular. People listen to them on public transport, in cars, while walking. They are good for sick people, older people, little people, active people, blind people, and people who are just sick of looking at a screen.

Some audio books do exceedingly well.

It is also, however, exceedingly expensive.

Why?

Because you have to pay the narrator. Audio books fall or

stand with the quality of their production and the voice of the narrator. Therefore it can hurt you to go with a cheap narrator. People won't like the production, they will give bad reviews, and you won't recoup your investment.

Audio files are generally paid for per finished hour. This is the length of the file once it's for sale. The good narrators generally ask $300 per hour for their work. Each hour of the finished product typically takes them 4–5 hours to produce. An average book is 9–10 hours long.

This is to illustrate that it's not cheap.

There are not half the number of promotional tools available for promoting audio books as there are for ebooks. But if you promote the ebook, the audio book will get sales, too.

Still, I don't advocate doing audio books until you can afford to lose the money. Not that you will, but it might take you quite a while to recoup.

Translations

Some writers have ventured into having their books translated into other languages. This may be a viable option, especially if you know there is a market for your genre in that language. It's a huge benefit if you're familiar with that market or you can hire the help of someone who is. For this reason, I suggest that translations are something to consider once you're out of the beginner stage.

Knowing the market is hugely important. A well-known writer in the self-publishing community paid to have his books translated. The books sold well in English, so why not? The translated books sold very little. The problem? He wrote "prepper" fiction and no one who is not in the US even knows what that is.

So: do your research.

If you decide to go ahead with it, there are a few options:

♦ Going with a translation site, like Babelcube. They're like an aggregator for translated books. They have price structures to pay the translators. Cons: how do you check the quality of the translation?

♦ Paying a translator outright. In some European countries, there are laws that force you to do a royalty share with them. You can't just pay and be done with it, unless you find a translator of a European language who does not live in Europe. Cons: this is an obvious minefield. Also, how to advertise in a language you don't speak?

♦ Find a publisher to do it for you. A publisher in the country where they sell should be familiar with how to advertise and where to sell. They will eat the translation costs and hopefully recoup them from sales. Cons: you may be required to sign a contract handing them the rights for a number of years. The publisher "should" know how to market, but it doesn't necessarily mean that they will.

Large print

Most people who are vision impaired have gone to e-readers. You can enlarge the font without having to purchase an expensive and heavy book. As added incentive, few books are available in large print.

But it may be worthwhile doing a large print edition of your book when your book appeals specifically to those who typically read large print and you know how to reach them.

PDF files

Once you start accumulating a mailing list, you will occasionally get requests from people for PDF files.

Should you make your book available in PDF?

On the one hand, it doesn't need to cost you much, if you know how to convert it.

On the other . . . if pirates are going to offer your book, it's always in PDF. I don't worry too much about piracy, but don't want to hand them my book on a platter either.

Whether you do it or not, think about it: Amazon and the major retailers don't offer PDFs. So: the people who ask for PDFs are unlikely to buy your books anyway.

To-do list:

- ◆ Consider what other formats are available and whether you are or may become interested in them

- ◆ Sign up to some service providers to get their emails on the latest news

Aaaarghhh! Here Come The Pirates!

MANY NEW WRITERS are dismayed to find their books pirated only a few days after them have published them.

They come to forums, upset, wondering what to do about it.

Some people advocate sending DMCA take-down notices, but I usually tell them don't worry about it.

Why not? And why do I recommend ignoring Google Alert messages about your books being available on sites where you haven't authorised them to be? I even say: don't click that link!

Well, in the first place these sites are rarely legit. If you have virus software installed, it will often go berserk when going to these sites.

That's because they try to infect your computer. This is the main aim of the site: to install a Trojan on your computer. So: Rule 1: don't even click that link.

If you did click the link, you'll find, in at least 90% of the cases, that they don't actually have your book. They've downloaded the sample from a retailer and have put that up. In order to get the rest of the book, you have to either join the site or hand over your credit card details, at which point—surprise, surprise!—your computer will freeze up and you'll have to wipe the viruses off.

These are phishing sites. They don't sell books. They collect credit cards.

In the small percentage of cases where the site does have your book and people can download it freely, think about who would visit such a site:

♦ People who like to read but have no money.

♦ People who possess the level of geekery necessary to sideload a file and not import embedded viruses on their computer. In other words: smart people with no money.

♦ People who believe everything on the Internet should be free.

The first two groups have a habit of getting good jobs later in life, and with a good job comes the willingness to pay for ease of access. One click, and it's on your phone, tablet, e-reader and laptop. They'll pay $5 for that no problem, once they've finished their degree.

The last group: you'll never sell anything to them, but they may become fans and recommend your books to their friends.

In fact, I try to lure those people into my ARC team, where they get my books for free if they write reviews. They can turn into very loyal and thankful readers.

To-do list:

- If you want to go this route, find a standard text for a DMCA takedown notice and paste it in a template in your email programme

- Or simply disable Google Alerts and ignore pirates (I highly recommend this option)

Do These Things

ADVICE. AS ANY WOMAN who has ever been pregnant will know, the world is full of unsolicited advice. Once you put a book out there, you will attract no end of it.

Many people are going to want to give you advice, and many will even try to charge you money for it. You will get advice such as "Self-publishing ruins your career prospects" (yes, people like that still exist), or "You need an editor," oddly accompanied by the notification that the giver of advice is, in fact, an editor, and probably a pretty poor one at that.

People will tell you to write this or that genre, or not to write this or that genre. They will tell you to get more reviews, as if that alone will make your books sell better, or to enter prize competitions.

In the endless morass of advice you will get, only a few things are important:

- If you asked for the advice, it's 1000 times more valuable than if it was given unasked.

- If the giver of the advice benefits personally from the advice, discard it immediately.

- If it sounds like something that you, with your skill set, are willing or able to do and it doesn't cost a huge mount of time, then try it.

- If you find something that works, then do more of that.

- If something doesn't work, stop doing it.

How do you determine what works?

All this requires that you have a pretty solid idea of how well your books sell as a result of actions taken by you. Keeping records of what you sell and when is necessary to please your accountant, but it is also useful for checking the effectiveness of ads or other promotional activities.

Some people make a study of data and do amazing and pretty things with it, but for someone who would rather write, some fairly basic bookkeeping will do.

Things I like to record:

- A rolling total of sales over 30 days, to check if overall sales are trending up or down.

- Total sales per book over the current financial year and over the lifetime of the book.

There is no number wizardry necessary to obtain these records. All retailers allow you to define the time period over which they give data. I simply keep an eye on the 30-day moving total.

Once a month I download all the spreadsheets from all retailers and feed them into a program called Trackerbox. It's PC only (actually the single most important reason I still have a PC).

Some people use their own spreadsheets. There is also a web-based program called Booktrakr. I'm personally uncomfortable with giving an app all my passwords to the retailer sites, but I know quite a few people use it.

I guess I'll have to say something about the schnazzy app called Book Report that's used by a number of authors. It's free if you sell less than $1000 per month on Amazon, and $10 per month if you sell more. To be honest, it's pretty, but utterly useless to me, because I need something that handles all retailers, not just Amazon.

At the very basic level you can add up titles and monthly sales in a simple spreadsheet.

In any case, do this, track your monthly sales per retailer and per title, because it is your most important vehicle for checking if your money and time spent on promotions is spent wisely.

No one can tell you with certainty that a promotion is going to work. You can only check this for yourself. Check it, because if it doesn't work, stop doing it. Stop wasting your time and money on stuff that doesn't work.

To-do list:

♦   Set up a system that tracks sales and allows you to see how much you're selling on a daily, monthly or yearly basis. Mostly this will involve some type of accounting software or spreadsheet

Four Steps To Stardom

IT WAS A LITTLE WHILE AGO that bestselling romance writer Courtney Milan wrote her famous "Regions of Discoverability" post on the Kindleboards.

In a nutshell, it defines four stages in a writer's career:

Stage 1, where no one knows you, you have perhaps one or a couple of books out, and everything seems an uphill battle: not just selling books, but getting reviews and getting people to sign up for your mailing list. Literally everything. Promotions are hard. You get a little spike but the sales go back to the same level the day after, and that level is pretty much nothing. You struggle to sell a book a day, or earn more than $100 per month from your writing. You feel there must be something you're doing wrong: maybe I'm not spending enough on ads, maybe my covers suck, maybe my books suck.

At *stage 2*, a writer becomes more well-known, and sales

grow, as well as effectiveness of advertising. People comment that there is often not that much time between reliably selling $100 per month and selling $1000 per month. When you're doing this, obviously something is going right. You will have more books, people will be familiar with your series, and you are likely to have more than one. Because readers see that you have complete series, they know that you're not going to abandon them. Maybe they've seen your name somewhere before. Promotions become more effective.

At *stage 3*, quite a few people know who you are. You don't need to push advertising so much anymore, because a new release will sell itself. Your audience will be your most important sales vehicle.

At *stage 4*, the retailers will know who you are and will give you special promotions. You will have reps at the retailers.

The hardest part, of course, is getting out of stage 1. You're advertising your socks off, nothing works, everything seems an uphill struggle. You're publishing new books to a very small audience. You may get a small bump in sales, but it's not lasting.

Don't fear, most of us have been there. And yes, it's not easy, but this is where you put your head down and keep writing your series. Stop the series that sell the worst, expand on the series that people like best. Give the readers more of what they like.

. . . and this is essentially what this book is about. More books, consistent output, more readers. Rinse and repeat.

We're now going to talk about how to advertise your book. But first I want to kill another myth . . .

The Biggest Myth In The History Of Publishing

A VERY PERSISTENT myth out there says that reviews sell books. There is a pretty graphic that goes with it, exhorting people to review books for their favourite authors, because once the book has fifty reviews, Amazon will start promoting it for the author. You will see it rehashed every so often, especially by traditionally published authors, on either Facebook or Twitter.

It's bunk.

Of course it is true that authors very much appreciate reviews, and that reviewing their books is a nice service you can extend to the authors whose books you read.

But the statement that Amazon will promote a book that has fifty reviews?

It's bunk.

It's utter, complete bunk.

The fact that people believe this rubbish is one of the reasons that services exist where you can buy reviews. Remember John Locke?

So what is the relationship between reviews and sales? Do reviews sell books?

What really sells a book is social proof. If people see that so many people have commented on a book, more people will buy it. But you must understand that this is a function of the book having sold a lot in the first place.

How do you get reviews?

Reviews are a function of sales. The more books you sell, the more reviews you get. The more reviews you have, the more books you will have sold. A good ballpark figure for likely reviews is: one review for every 100 sales, one review for every 1000 free downloads. Want more reviews? Get selling! Lower your price, run some promotions, give your books to anyone who wants them. Don't badger them for reviews, but simply mention that you would love a review.

How else do you get reviews?

The best trick to get reviews was pointed out to me by a friend of mine, Carolynn Gockel. She said: every time you get a review, put a thank you message on Facebook and Twitter. No need to mention the reviewer in person—they might be embarrassed—just say thank you for another review. That's it! No begging, just saying thank you.

Using ARCs

Advanced Reader Copies are a powerful way to get reviews, but you first need a mailing list and some readers. Ask people on your list if they would like to get the book free if they write a review. Keep them in a separate mailing list. Bookfunnel has a paid option where you can make sure that only the people on this list can download the book. It's called "Midlist with Integrations". Give these people the download link to the book a couple of weeks before the book goes live.

On Amazon, do the following: Put up the book for pre-order a week or two before the live date, and don't tell anyone about it (aka "secret preorder"). A few days later, publish the print version. Once Createspace has put up the print book, the book will now be officially available for purchase and your reviewers can post their reviews, even if they can't buy the ebook, and the print book is not going to be delivered until the official release date.

Personally, I don't make too much fuss over whether they post a review or not, although the integration with Bookfunnel allows me to see who has downloaded the books and I should be able to tell who has reviewed from my Amazon page. I may choose to do something with that information later. At this point in time, I don't.

Your Life's Work Is In Your Hands

WHEN WRITING FOUR novels a year, you are constantly adding to your inventory of intellectual property. After thee years of work, you will have twelve books that you can sell in many different forms, on many different platforms, for as long as you like. This body of work is your capital that makes you your income.

This is the very important concept that goes hand in hand with the rest of the Three-Year Plan. You keep working on your overall intellectual property, and you keep doing things that keep those books selling.

A body of work is your stock in your virtual shop. You need to nurture it, look after it, give it a new lick of paint every now and then, and you need to make sure that it presents a unified picture.

People need to be able to see, at a single glance, which books go together. The collection of books on your bookshelf needs to look pretty.

Covers can't look too dated, the formatting has to be adapted if new formatting options arise, and your links in front and back matter should be kept updated.

A catalogue of books requires maintenance.

It requires a clean brand.

The word brand is, of course, very much a marketing word; and it's on the receiving end of a fair bit of ridicule from the "I write for my art" crowd. But a brand is no more than graphic elements that allow a casual observer to tell that the book in question is yours and that it belongs to a certain series.

Think about it by imagining that you were walking into a fashion store. If half of the clothes on the racks were for teens and the other half were geared towards women over 60, then you'd feel weirded out.

You wouldn't buy at a shop that sold widely different items for no good reason, so why should authors present their output as vastly varied? This applies especially when you write across very different genres and have books of varying length that are not in series.

It's a fine balance to find between lumping too much together and fragmenting your catalogue too much. If genres are very different then it may be worth going with a pen name. However for each pen name you will have to do double the work in maintaining a website, mailing list and advertising. Is it going to be worth the effort? That is something you will have to decide for yourself.

I have always resisted splitting up my work for this reason. If you have trouble sending regular updates to your mailing list when you have one list, just think about what your work is going to be like for two pen names.

To-do list:

♦   Decide on your brand and communicate this clearly to your cover designer

♦   Put evaluation, and upgrades if necessary, on your calendar

Platform And Social Media

YOU WILL OFTEN hear marketers talking about the term platform. What they mean is how many followers you have on the various social media sites, like Facebook, Twitter, Instagram and the like. Also how many people read your blog or are on your mailing list.

But I hear you say—gulp—I don't have a mailing list, and I use Facebook for my friends and I don't understand Twitter. Is that a bad thing? Do I have to become one of those horrible writers shouting Buy My Book on Twitter?

No. In fact I recommend that you don't become one of those writers. There are quite enough of them already. Also, most of those those writers don't really understand how Twitter works.

Much as it might sadden you, your social media engagement can be quite important. It is not how people buy your book, but it is certainly how people find out about you. If you entertain them on those platforms, it's more likely that they will eventually buy your books.

But you have to be engaging and post stuff that they are interested in reading.

You don't have to do all of it.

But do set up accounts on each of the social media platforms. Make those accounts different from your personal account if you already have a personal account talking about other topics that have nothing to do with books. On Facebook, make an author page and don't use your personal profile.

Decide which social media site you're most comfortable with. Don't try to do all of them, because you'll end up tiring yourself out and being effective on none of them.

Say you like Facebook.

Post something on your page every day or at least a few times a week. It could be something about the book you're currently writing, something about a movie you saw, a book you read, or it could be about your rabbits. People love animals, so the rabbit post will probably win in engagement hands down. If you don't want to go to Twitter to post the same thing there, there are ways to set up that posts are shared on a number of social media sites. Tools like Hootsuite can help with this. Wordpress blogs have the option to post updates about new posts on a range of social media sites. Use them.

If a platform allows you to have a sticky post that people will always see when they visit your profile, use it to give a link to your website or mailing list signup page.

Whatever you choose to do, reply to comments you get. Social media is about engagement. It has to be fun and relaxing. No point doing something if you hate it.

Now if you regularly engage with people on social media, those people will be much more likely to buy your books or even recommend them to others. This is how social media works.

Don't want to do it? There are other ways of becoming known to readers.

To-do list:

♦   Make accounts on social media separate from your personal accounts

♦   Set up a Facebook author page

♦   Set up an author Twitter account

♦   Choose which platform you're going to use most

♦   Set up cross-posting from that platform to the ones you don't plan on using

A Word About Goodreads

GOODREADS IS A social media platform based around reading. On it, you can place books on virtual bookshelves and post reviews, comment on reviews made by other people, create or vote in book lists, join reading groups and friend people.

The question whether there is any point in a writer investing time into Goodreads is one that often comes up on forums.

The Goodreads reader community can come down like a tonne of bricks on any writer who self-promotes too much, or who infiltrates groups for the sole reason of promoting.

Goodreads gets the rap for being nasty, but it merely reflects the general feel in the community: nobody likes people who constantly self-promote. Nobody likes the author who goes ballistic online about a bad review. Goodreads is just extraordinarily good at ridiculing those writers.

For one, Goodreads is a community for readers to talk about books. Many of those readers feel uncomfortable when the author of said book is looking over their shoulder. So tread with care.

Join Goodreads as a reader, not a writer. Join groups to talk about books you've read. There are corners where you can announce your freebies or new books. Stick to these places if you want to promote at all.

The minimum things you should do on Goodreads is to claim your author profile and make sure your books are linked. Goodreads is owned by Amazon, so if you put a book up on Amazon it will automatically find its way to your Goodreads page.

Another very useful and low-maintenance thing you can do on Goodreads is to syndicate your blog, so that blog posts show up on the site.

You Must Advertise

ONCE YOU HAVE a decent set of products, for example you have completed a series of three books and have started another, about a year or so into the plan, you should start to think more seriously about advertising.

Note that I don't think it is necessarily wrong to start advertising earlier, but I would also caution against not spending too much effort or money, unless something works really well, and then of course, do more of it as I said earlier (but not to the exclusion of writing).

Sometimes new writers get sucked into the notion that they need to "launch" their first books with a lot fanfare, without having an audience to fanfare to, and without having a clear idea where to spend their money. They buy expensive ads and try to mimic traditionally published book launches, forgetting that the publishing industry sells to bookshops, not to customers, and that the purpose of a traditional book launch is to impress first and sell second.

It is also very easy to spend a lot of money on ads that don't work, like newspaper or magazine ads and pay per click advertising.

Even if you have a very large budget, it's often hard to find where to spend money effectively. Sure, it's easy enough to blow huge amounts of money on Facebook ads and Google Adwords, but they're unlikely to be very effective if you've never done this before.

Things that traditional publishers rely on—print ads, radio slots, interviews and print reviews—don't actually have much effect at all. People don't read about a book in a print newspaper and then go to the effort of searching for where they can buy it online.

Effective advertising opportunities are extremely rare. As an independent writer, you are usually presented with the following broad advertising options:

Listing services

These are websites that, for a fee, will post your book for a discounted price to their list of subscribers. Some of these are reasonably effective, especially, at the time of writing, Bookbub, Ereader News Today, Freebooksy, Book Barbarian, Robin Reads and Booksends. New sites come up and drop off all the time, so find out which are the best sites at the Writer's Cafe at the Kindleboards (have you noticed that this is my standard answer to all these types of questions?)

Note that most of those sites are unlikely to give you an immediate return on investment, unless your book is the first in a longer series. Most charge anywhere from $5 to $70, which, in terms of bang for buck, makes them reasonably expensive compared to the hallowed and pricey Bookbub, which almost never fails to make you money, sometimes significantly more than the (quite steep) fees. Bookbub is by far the best bang for your buck, even if to start with you have to shell out a lot of bucks.

If you hear of a new site that you've never heard of before, check them out. Look to see how easily people can sign up as readers. Look at the sales rankings of some of the most recently advertised books. Check the site's Alexa rankings for an independent verification for how many people come to the site.

Pay per click/display ads

These are Facebook ads, Twitter ads, Adwords and a whole raft of similar services, where you pay (and often bid) for the display of your ad or clicks on the ad.

This option is not for wimps and it's not for people who fear losing money on experiments. Often it takes quite a lot of experimenting to get ads working, and then they might still be too expensive. You often end up bidding against people with more expensive product to sell than a $3 book, and they can afford to pay much more per click.

If you're interested in this option, I advise doing some research on how to best set up your ads. You can find a lot of information on the Internet, or you can take a course. Crime writer Mark Dawson offers a set of three introductory videos that are an excellent primer to Facebook ads for self-published writers. He also offers some courses. While they are not cheap, I can state that I utterly respect Mark and that he acts with the utmost integrity. How much you will get out of his courses depends on your level of knowledge and the level of commitment you're willing to make.

From my perspective the problem is that making pay-per-click advertising work for you takes time, often a lot of it. Then there is the maintaining of ads and constant creation of new ones, as well as the regular scramble whenever an advertiser suddenly pulls the rug on ads that worked well.

Would you be better off spending that time writing? That's something you'll have to answer for yourself before going down this route. I suspect, for many writers, the answer will be yes. I would not recommend it as something for beginners.

Cross-promotion with other authors

These are activities where you pool resources, in this case your social media reach, to pull in more people interested in books. This works very well if promotions are genre-targeted, and where all participants write fairly similar books.

The best promotions are those you do with friends and that are not run by a promotional site. The downside is that it usually requires some work from your side, and for it to work you need to have some level of social media footprint already. If you can find no cross-promotions to join, you can make your own. All you need are a couple of friends whose work you respect who have a decent social media presence that's different from yours. You can make the promotion a group sale, where you all reduce one of your books to 99c and put them on a page where people can see the promotion and click through to the buy links. Or you could bundle the books into a set and sell it cheaply or give it away for free. You will need a cover and someone will need to format the file. But there are also several bundling options available if you don't want to do this yourself: check out Bookfunnel and Bundlerabbit.

But the last method of advertising is the most powerful of all, and I'll devote an entire section to it: your mailing list.

But first let me remind you . . .

To-do list:

- ♦ Investigate the best bang-for-your-buck promotion sites for your genre

- ♦ Look at their requirements

- ♦ Look at promo results and Alexa rankings of all smaller sites before booking

- ♦ Inform yourself about Facebook ads before trying to run any

- ♦ Join author cross-promotion groups

Work Is A Four-Letter Word

THERE ARE AS MANY paths to achieving your publishing aims as there are writers, even if that aim is making a living from your writing. Without fail, all of those paths involve work. A lot of hard, consistent work.

People who do work regularly and who try consistently and stubbornly always prevail over the ones who don't. Even if, at the beginning, the work mostly leads to failure; and make no mistake—it usually does.

If things don't go the way you want and your sales are poor, get some advice from a few people you trust, readjust whatever needs readjusting and keep working.

A big discussion is perpetually going on in the self-publishing world as to whether publishing success is determined by luck. On the one hand there are those who say that all their success is due to their own hard work; on the other there are those who complain that at the time that others found success, things were easier or they got lucky.

It's a bit of both.

But without a good product, you will never get lucky. Without your constant involvement in activities where readers can find you, it's unlikely they ever will.

A great example of this is Bookbub.

Considered the holy grail of paid advertising, you would have to work hard to make a Bookbub featured ad a failure. They virtually always turn a positive return on your investment, most frequently many times over.

Because writers know this, their ad slots are heavily over-subscribed. In short: it's hard to get accepted into a promotion. You can get lucky and be accepted on the first try (there is that word luck again), but most writers don't. In fact, I think I had at least fifteen to twenty rejections before I was accepted, and I've had an average of one acceptance for every seven submissions since.

So no, I'm not lucky to have been accepted. I know the odds are small, and I'm stubborn about it. I was published in the big trade-publishing magazines, where the acceptance rate is like 3%, and mostly by pre-booked or invited big-name writers, and I know it's about sheer stubborn persistence. If a submission gets rejected, send something else. If you have nothing else, send it again as soon as you can. Don't fall down the trap of overanalysing the rejection notice: it's likely a canned email. Just submit again, and again, and again.

I make sure I have the nicest-looking book possible and keep trying.

Up until very recently, I only did Bookbub featured ads for free books. Not that this is all I submitted—it's what they took. But in October last year, I was accepted for a paid ad for the omnibus of the three books of the *Icefire Trilogy*. It did really well, and sold over 3000 copies on Amazon on that day, plus at least 1000 on other platforms. The book went to 32 on the overall Amazon chart.

Up until this part, the story is the hard work and persistence sort.

But now comes the luck part: it didn't go back down below 2000 for months. In fact, it stuck in the top 200 in the UK for a long time.

Why?

I could be snooty and say I simply wrote a good book, but I think it has more to do with being in the right place at the right time. Yes, it requires a good element of luck. The book would have done well, but I had no control over it doing that well.

In order to achieve this type of luck, however, you need to work hard and position your books in a place where they can occasionally be taken up by luck and carried to heights where you don't normally reside. But when you have reached those heights once, it become easier to reach them again.

There is a saying that lucky breaks most often happen to people who don't need them, and this is indicative of what you need to do. You have to make sure that you don't need the lucky break in order to survive. You also need to put yourself out in places where luck can find you. You never know where that may be, so try as many things as possible at least once.

Mailing Lists

THE AUTHOR MAILING LIST!

I would personally consider it the most undervalued and underused tool in the author's promotional toolkit.

I started using email mailing lists in 2000, when you could still simply collect email addresses of your business contacts and email them regularly without having to ask for permission, without having them sign up and without mandatory unsubscribe options.

In fact, none of the services offering all these things existed. I ran an online non-fiction bookstore, and I would buy batches of specialist books from estates of the deceased, then send the inventory to the 150-odd people on my list. They were rare and often very expensive books. I'd sell hundreds of dollars worth of books within an hour. It was magic!

Of course then Amazon came along and flooded the market with of some of these books, while the ones that were truly rare became completely unobtainable, and the gold rush ended.

I went into other things and forgot about how well the mailing list used to work until the issue of mailing lists became a hot topic in the author sphere. At that point, a lot of authors were using their mailing list as a back-end service only. The idea that one could use a list to actively advertise and sell, and invest in a mailing list in lieu of advertising, is still quite new to some people.

UK crime writer Mark Dawson has an empire that he has built entirely on the back of an aggressive email list strategy.

The mailing list is your most powerful sales strategy. The people on the list are yours, they have either read your books or have given you permission to try and sell them your books. So, sell them books!

How?

In the next section, I will list the basic things you need to set up a mailing list.

How To Set It Up

SO, HOW DO YOU set up a mailing list?

There are several things you will need:

♦ In the first place, you should sign up with a mailing list provider, a third party website that hosts your list and deals with subscriber vetting and unsubscribes.

♦ Then you need somewhere to set up your information that you will use in your emails. This will most likely be your website.

♦ You will need a way for subscribers to sign up. Most likely, this will be a form, preferably on your website. It is important that you won't need to change this form frequently. Preferably, you will never change this link.

♦   You will need to know how and where you will get your subscribers. If you want them to have read at least one of your books, get them from links in the back of a book (but notice how I told you to also put the link in the front of the book?)

♦   You will need a plan; what are you going to do with this list and what are you going to send these people? Is it a chatty newsletter? What will you talk about? Any particular subjects? Will you talk about your books, about writing, about the background information relating to your books, or research you did for the books? Will you review books in your genre and talk about those? The list is endless. But it's best to define a brand and a style, and stick to it.

♦   You will also need some graphics that you want to use as a header. This could be as simple as a photo of yourself, or a graphic that includes your books. It's worth spending some money on this, because this header will be your brand.

In all, setting up a list is quick and easy. Sign up for an account, make a signup form and you're done! But setting up a list for maximum benefit will take a bit of thought and planning.

The next section will cover the basics of mailing list operation. There is a lot more to be said about how to run your list, how to get people to subscribe and how to engage them. This is covered in book 2 of this series, *Mailing Lists Unboxed*.

Where To Host Your List

IF YOU WANT to have a mailing list, by far the easiest way is to sign up with a company that provides mailing list hosting. Yes, it is true that they are unlikely to be free forever, but many of them have free plans for low numbers or for a limited time.

At the time of writing, the options used by many writers are:

- Mailerlite. Free plan for up to 1000 subscribers. Excellent help service, although their English may leave a bit to be desired. Mailerlite is based in Lithuania and their help team is from all over the world. I use them and they're awesome.

- Mailchimp. Free plan for up to 2000 subscribers. Cost climbs very quickly after that. Pretty lousy help service, even if on a paid plan.

- Convertkit. Expensive, but offers extensive tagging

options that some people really like.

♦   Aweber. Fairly similar to Mailchimp, except there is no free plan.

Whatever you do, unless you really know what you're doing, please ignore the voice of your little tech-savvy cousin: you are highly unlikely to be able to run your mailing list from your self-hosted WordPress site. It's not that it's impossible— larger marketing companies run their lists with custom software from their own servers and it's not technically difficult— but doing so carries a huge number of risks that you will be unaware of as beginner, let alone know how to avoid, such as:

Risk #1: Having your account and website cancelled

Spam is huge. In today's situation where your Internet service provider catches most of it, nobody even realises how huge. It used to be that domain owners were subjected to the full brunt of it. I could tell you about the day I received over 1000 spam emails, most of them in Arabic, but the expletives would send this book to the "adult" dungeon. Take it from me: the vast, vast majority of spam is caught before it ever reaches your inbox. The Internet is hypersensitive to anything that looks like spam.

So how does this risk affect a private author with a small list? After all, all you want to do is email some people about your new release?

Well, how does sending 2000 emails from a private email address sound? There are cheery plug-ins you can get, for free even, that will manage your newsletter. They will do as advertised, but please use this option for very small newsletters only, not the type I'm talking about.

Every Internet service provider has guidelines for banning spam or what looks like spam, or anything that could get them into hot water. That's why they don't want you sending thousands of emails from their servers, and why your account may get cancelled if you do.

Risk #2: Having your emails end up in people's spam folders or never be delivered

Now I have to say one thing: there will always be some of this happening. It's pretty much unavoidable. If it happens to someone who complains about it, ask them to use a different email address. This will almost always solve the problem.

Of course having your account cancelled is much more serious than your emails getting stuck in spam folders, but the effect is pretty much the same: people don't get your emails. Fortunately, there are some things you can do to avoid landing in the spam folder. Avoid using trigger words in the subject line (like FREE). Be specific with the email subject line so that people know what they're going to get. Don't try to be clever, because if people don't understand the message, they won't open. If they don't open, the email software will assume they're not interested and will automatically move the next email messages to spam.

Another thing you can do is to avoid using your free email provider address (like Gmail or Yahoo) as your "From:" address. Because many real spammers use free email addresses, this is often automatically a red flag.

Manage your list at a reputable email list service, which does its best to maintain the highest possible relevance rating for its customers. These companies have servers that are especially geared up to send huge quantities of email in a short period and not get flagged for sending spam.

In evaluating what company to choose, consider your current and future needs. Consider whether you are going to use your list as a service to existing readers or aggressively recruit email addresses and look at the company's price structure. Consider whether they have a free trial number of subscribers, and what level of automation they offer if they have a free subscriber level.

Consider how integrated they are with services you use to gather subscribers, like Facebook, your website or Instafreebie. Do they transport email addresses straight from Facebook or Instafreebie to your list or are you going to have to import CSV files?

Choose wisely according to your future budget, because moving a list is a major pain in the behind.

There are basically two types of email services: those that offer the full gamut of services, with an accordingly high price tag, like MailChimp, AWeber and ConvertKit, and those that are more basic like MailerLite and SendinBlue.

Let's be clear: by its very nature, the business of being an author is a simple business. The vast majority of authors don't run web stores with their own content delivery, nor would it make sense for authors to do this.

Why not?

Because if you can tickle the algorithms of a retailer site, the site can do the advertising for you, for as long as your book is highly ranked. If you sell books from your own site, you won't get any additional push from retailers. Remember this: they make money when you sell your book, so they have an interest in keeping you selling.

Now this may change in the future, but I've yet to see an author list that makes effective use of the high-end services offered by the full-service email list providers. For example, we will never be able to say whether or not a person we have directed to a retailer website has actually bought the book, because the retailers don't share that information. So why use a list service that offers that integration with web stores, and pay through the nose for services you will never use?

What you need is:

♦ The capability of producing all types of signup forms, including the ability to embed the form on your website.

♦ The ability to segment or group subscribers.

♦ Basic automation that triggers when a subscriber signs up.

Functionalities I strongly recommend considering:

♦ Automation based on parameters other than when they signed up, like when a subscriber clicks a link.

♦ Automation that puts subscribers on different lists and unsubscribes them based on actions in a chain of events.

In my personal view, it is absolutely unnecessary to sign up with an expensive blue ribbon service. I won't name names, but I initially used such a service, because there were not as many options when I started. When it got to the point that I was paying $140 per month for 12,000 subscribers, I jumped ship. I now pay $940 per year for 50,000 subscribers for exactly the same functionality, simply because I could not use the first service's sales reporting tools that I was paying for.

The current service doesn't offer a lot of those high-end integrations. That's fine. I can't use them anyway.

To-do list:

♦   Consider your needs for a mailing list now and in the future.

♦   Look at companies' options. Ask other writers what they use and why.

♦   Get an account at the provider of your choice.

Signup Forms

ONCE YOU'VE SET UP your account on the provider of your choice, you will need a signup form. You may also need some landing pages.

Now, you understand what a signup form is, but what's a landing page?

In short, a landing page is a page that focuses on one issue or item. It's a page where you send people to see an ad. The single function of a landing page can be for people to sign up, or it can be about ONE single book. At the bottom of the page, there is a link to buy the book. There are no other links on the page. No distracting menus, no links to other posts. This page is about this one single issue only, and if a visitor doesn't click the buy button, the only other way to get out is to close the tab.

The reason you send people to a landing page rather than

a regular page on your website is that you don't want them to become distracted, and you don't want the design of your page to distract from the reason they clicked on the link. A landing page is specifically designed to display that single item in a way that a web page is not. On a web page, you might have sidebars, a header and footer all cluttering up the page.

How do you make forms and landing pages?

Most providers will make pretty forms for you. Many will even offer the option of making landing pages. I strongly recommend AGAINST using these. Why? Because you will advertise these forms and pages wide. The links will be in your books. If you ever decide to change provider (a massive pain in the behind already), those forms are owned by them. You cancel the account, you lose the form. OK, OK, you can just make a new form at the new provider.

Yup, but what about all those 20,000 books you gave away in your last free Bookbub promotion, which all still have the old link in them?

Oops.

At the very least, use a link redirect through SmartURL or the plug-in prettylinks for WordPress. Services like those will provide you with a dummy URL that points to another URL that you can edit later.

Better still, of course, is to self-host the form.

By self-hosting the form I mean put the code somewhere on a page you own. This means that if you wanted to change your list or your provider, you only need to change the stuff on the page, not the page's URL.

How does this work?

Make a form for the list on your email provider's site, then copy the form's code (mostly through the "embed" option and paste the code into your website.

You often have various design options, from a full form with added text and pictures to a "slim" design, which consists only of the form fields and a "subscribe" button.

Hint: this and the WordPress plug-in prettylinks won't work if you're on a free blog platform.

This is why you really need a website.

Guess what the next chapter is about?

To-do list:

♦ Make one or more forms so that people can sign up to your list

♦ Embed this form in a page on your website—don't use the URL given by your provider

About Websites

ONE OF THE first things you are going to need to set up in order to have a successful mailing list is a website.

I mean a proper website, not one of these free blog jobs from WordPress or BlogSpot. Why? Because some things you need to do you can't do on free websites. If you're really cash-strapped, do get a free WordPress site, but make upgrading it to a self-hosted site a priority.

What is the main function of your website?

If you said *To display your books* you'd be only halfway right.

In the three-year plan method, the most important function of your website is that it forms a place where you can send people. It's a place where you can host your landing pages independent of retailers or other places that control who visits.

If you don't think this is important, consider Facebook.

Not so long ago, when you posted on Facebook, every one of your friends would see it. If you had an author page, all the people who had liked your page would see it.

These days, you can be lucky if a mere 10% of the people who have liked your page will see the update. If you want all of them to see it, you have to pay.

If you have invested a lot of time and money into getting likes on Facebook, you have a good reason to feel duped by Facebook. They can, with a few lines of code on their website, ruin the audience reach you've spent years to build up. Or they can go out of fashion. Remember Myspace?

So the three-year plan avoids the Facebooks of the world. It doesn't allow companies that have control over who sees your material to serve as an important link in the chain of contact between you and your reader.

This is the function of your website. It's a home to put things you want people to see, where you, and no one else, controls who sees it.

Of course, your website should contain pages for each of your books, but it should also contain sections where you can send people in your mailing list automation sequence. This can be landing pages for your books, but also interesting blog posts, cross-promotion sales, additional information about books, and even registration-only member sites. The possibilities are endless.

At the very least, your website should host your forms and your landing pages.

So, landing pages.

There are all sorts of programs you can buy to generate your landing pages. Most of them are subscription services (URGH!) and they do far more than you will ever need as author. So here is a hack for reasonably computer-literate people:

Go into your website's directory using your ISP's file menu. Create a new directory. Mine is called "pages".

Go to your ISP's app directory, and find WordPress. Install WordPress, but tell it to install the software in the directory you have just created, not in the root directory. This won't affect your normal website at all.

Then when it's completed, log into your new sub-site, go to the WordPress free theme directory and find a theme that allows you to turn off everything: the header, the footer, the menu, sidebars, post titles, post dates, commenting, social icons, EVERYTHING. You want to be left with a blank page, maybe with a border. Make sure the theme is mobile-friendly. I use the theme Tempera for both my website (where I have all the stuff turned on) and my pages (where I have everything turned off). It's free. Then simply start creating pages. They can be pretty basic, or Tempera has a very easy box where you can add your custom CSS to make it look a little bit more fancy. But landing pages are simple by definition, so simple will do. Title, cover, blurb, buy buttons. That's all you need.

While some options for creating and maintaining landing pages will charge you $10 per month—including fancy stuff you'll never use—this costs NOTHING.

To-do list:

♦ Get a self-hosted website

♦ Create signup pages and landing pages for your books on your website

Automation

SO NOW I HAVE a list and a website, what about this thing called automation?

Automation is an action that happens according to a trigger you set in your mailing list provider's menu.

For example, when a subscriber joins a list, they automatically receive a welcome email in which you introduce yourself. If you give subscribers something for free, you would do it in this email.

Then, two weeks later, another email goes out automatically in which you ask them if they got the book and maybe ask them another question. Then two weeks later you might give them something else or send them another question.

I use this standard automation sequence on most of my lists. It requires none of my involvement and always runs in the background.

But there is much more you can do with automation. Because, in the third email, people get the option to click on a link that tells them that they'll be sent an introduction to my series, a different series every second week. It tells them that if they don't want to get it because they already know about my series, click here and Hey! They won't get those emails.

Meanwhile, another four automation sequences keep track of which people downloaded which of my free books. For each of those links, it makes a list of people and a set number of days later, sends them an email asking if they enjoyed the book, if they have any questions, if they'd like to review and introducing the second book in the series.

Meanwhile, in another list, I give people an option to click a link and they'll be automatically moved to another group. When they click, it automatically removes their name from the group and presents them with a form to enter an email address. It's called "change your address".

But, if people have been on my list for six months and have opened none of their emails, they'll get an email that says, "Here is a free book." If they don't open it, a month later they get another email that says, "Here is another book for you." And if they don't open that one either, they get an email that says, "Do you still want to be on this list?" At this point, the automation automatically unsubscribes the people. But if they click on the link "yes" they will see a form where they can enter their email address and resubscribe.

These are just a few examples to show that there are no limits to what you can do with automation.

A word of warning: designing complex automation will hurt your brain.

At the very least, I recommend that you have a short welcome sequence that introduces people to you and your work and that gives them a few free things.

I go into much more detail about automation in part 2 in this series, *Mailing Lists Unboxed*.

To-do list:

♦   Set up a basic automation email that welcomes new subscribers to your list

About Mandates

IT IS IMPORTANT to understand the ethics of operating mailing lists.

In this case, ethics means: people must understand what they're signing up for.

When signing up, you make them a promise, and you should stick to that promise. You shouldn't suddenly change the name and subject matter of your list.

You should never port lists from one author name to the next, or import mailing lists from other businesses, even businesses that you own.

If people haven't signed up for it, they have every right to be upset about being sent emails.

Every one of your emails should have an unsubscribe link that leads to a simple unsubscribe page, or, even easier, unsubscribes them with one click. People don't want to go through hassle to get off a list. They will report you for spam instead.

Even if you do all this, you will get plenty of people who don't remember signing up, or who didn't read the part that said that by signing up for a competition, they would end up on the authors' mailing lists.

When you operate a mailing list, you will soon find out that there are a lot of crazy people out there. Don't give them any more reason to go nuts than necessary. Define what you're going to do, stick to it and never import anyone who hasn't given their email address with the understanding that you will be emailing them.

To-do list:

♦   Decide what your list is for and write out what you'll promise people in their first email

You Are Not Your Own Target Audience

BUT, YOU WILL SAY, I hate mailing lists.

I hear you. Personally, I rarely sign up for them either. My in-box is full enough as it is.

But there are obviously people who like to sign up. They like getting deals, they like conversations. They may have more time than I do, or they just like to get email.

One of the most important things you have to realise: selling books successfully is not about you, the author, nor is it your personal preferences. It's about doing things that are proven to work.

Therefore, you must test a lot of things, even things that you as a person would never respond to.

Get this: you are not your own target audience. That's OK.

Plenty of people love being on mailing lists and love hearing from authors. Some people will be there because they're your fans. Some people will be there because you give out the occasional free book, and some will be there because they're lonely and like getting email. You can never know who is who.

Do what you said you would do when they joined your list, give them reasons to open the email and click links.

Remember to judge people primarily by their actions, not their words. Mailing list providers give you stats on who opens, who clicks what. A few loud people will email you all the time and complain, but your mailing list not about appeasing the few loud complainers. Watch online what the majority of them do.

Which links do they click most? Which emails with which titles do they open?

If something unexpected happens, try to find out why. Send them a survey. People love answering surveys and giving their opinions. Don't ask "What would you do?" but "What did you do?"

Questions like:

- ♦ Which authors do you like?

- ♦ Which genres do you read besides mine?

- ♦ Where do you buy your books?

- ♦ Which of my books have you read?

Especially the last question will surprise you. Authors frequently assume that people on their list have already read all their books. Most of them won't. So, make use of that fact. They're interested in you. Remind them that you have all these books. Use automation to do this.

Once you free yourself from the assumption that all these people's likes and dislikes are just like your own, there are no limits to how you can engage with these people who have told you, by signing up: "Entertain me."

Help, I'm F(l)ailing

HANG ON A MOMENT, I hear people say. I did everything you told me to do. I wrote books in series. I set up a website, started a mailing list and automation, did some cross-promotions and I now have 4000 people on my list. There is only one problem: they don't buy my books! They're just costing me money.

This happens from time to time, and it's never easy to treat or even diagnose when you can't see the whole process. Therefore you must continuously evaluate your results. But here are some common reasons that people continue to struggle:

They're impatient

I would give the whole process at least a year to start giving consistent results. If you give away free books, you need to give people the time to read them. Many people who download free books will have massive collections on their devices. They must be reminded a few times that your books are worth

154

a try. Your automated email sequence should do that.

But still, virtually no one reads a free book immediately. Give them time.

The ad copy does not draw them in

Because people have so many free books on their devices, they need to make a decision about what to read first. Only the truly anal people will read on a first-received, first-read basis. Most people will browse their libraries and will pick the book that they've heard most about or that sounds the most interesting. So it's not enough to give people a free book. You have to make them want to read that book.

Your blurb needs to be interesting. Whenever you mention your book in your emails, it needs to draw people in.

To be able to do this well is an art, and it's called copywriting. Grab a book or two about how to write ads, and about how to push people's buttons with words. You'll be glad that you did.

The book fails to deliver

This is the hardest thing for a writer to hear: the book just doesn't draw enough people into the series. How do you know that this might be the issue?

People buy book 1 but after a year, few have bought book 2, even when you've advertised a fair bit.

You're having a lot of trouble getting reviews, and a good proportion of the ones you do get are of the "meh" variety, or they mention specific issues, like characters being unlikeable or shallow, the ending being unbelievable or unsatisfactory or the plot being stodgy, slow or confusing.

The book has failed the basic rules of writing: don't bore the reader, don't confuse the reader, don't annoy the reader.

Ask advice from a developmental editor and make changes if you can. But mostly, your best investment is to use what you've learned in another series. Start something new. Make it slightly related to the rest of your work so that you maximise potential sell-through.

A note about cliffhangers

A cliffhanger is a book that ends on a major new reveal or a point of tension where the reader has to buy the next book to find out what happens. TV series are masters at cliffhangers.

At any one time, you can find any number of heated discussions about cliffhangers. That readers hate them and how much they hate them, and that they feel duped into buying the next book; that there are such things as "good" cliffhangers and "bad" cliffhangers, where the good ones supposedly resolve certain plots points, but the bad ones are only to dupe the reader into buying the next book.

Yadda yadda yadda yadda.

The only thing that counts is this: are people buying the next book? Have you made them feel enough that they click "Buy"? No matter how much they complain? No matter how angry they seem to be?

If the answer is yes, cliffhang away. If the answer is no, they probably never complain about your cliffhangers anyway, because they give up reading long before they get to the end.

Remember: at any one point in your career, if you strike a rough patch and try to figure out what to do about it, don't listen to what people say, other than, if you've judged that they're qualified to give you advice, watch what they do. Test, analyse, decide.

Don't be a circlejerk

When you're down on your luck and feel depressed about your sales and wonder what to do about it, you'll likely stumble across groups of like-minded authors who have devised various schemes to hold up the illusion of selling. They review and even buy each other's books.

Don't waste your time doing this stuff.

You only need to have made an ill-chosen return-review arrangement once to know that it's a bad, bad idea (that's aside from the fact that Amazon doesn't like it when authors review other authors). How so? Well, imagine you exchange reviews with someone and they read your book quickly and give it a glowing review. You, however, are busy and don't get to their book for a while. Then you open it and oh my, is it awful! What do you write in that review? Seriously, you do not want to be in a situation like this.

I'm not even going to talk about buying each other's books. That's just dumb, because, circlejerks aside, it's treating the symptoms, not the cause.

You're not selling as much as you like. A poor ranking and a lack of reviews are symptoms of poor sales, not the cause.

Readers are not stupid. They can pick a book with a high rank that's unlikely to have gained that rank fairly. They can pick canned reviews.

Propping up rank artificially and fishing for circlejerk reviews at best makes your book look odd to prospective buyers. At worst, Amazon will cancel your account.

If you're not selling and your next release is a while off, you can do these things, in increasing order of investment in time and money:

- Change the categories
- Do some marketing
- Change the cover
- Change your book's description
- Rewrite the beginning

Better still: write another book using all the stuff you've learned.

You Are The Secret Sauce

HERE IS A word of advice if you're new and feeling over-whelmed. You came into this writing gig because you loved telling stories, and now you're told that you need to do all this STUFF?

There is good news for you: writing a good story is still what sells you the most books. All the things I've discussed in this book are to augment the reader's experience of the books you write. They are designed to get the most out of the books you write and to set you up so that you don't have to spend 80% of your time running around yelling, "Buy my book!"

This is a note to make sure you understand that there is no secret sauce. No magic thing you can apply to your book that will make it start selling, other than to write an engaging book. In fact, you, dear author, are the secret sauce. But it's not a fast-working sauce, and it does not come with a ready-made recipe.

You often see that newer writers are very keen to get their books going as quickly as possible. They buy expensive ads, watch their rankings of their single book like a hawk, and panic when they don't sell as much as they want.

What are they doing wrong? Why aren't they having the success that is owed to them?

Well, they weren't writing their next book, for starters. They got suckered down the rabbit hole by some big name author uttering that launch is important.

It is, sort of.

It's actually a lot more important if you're a traditionally published author, because your book gets a six-week window in which it has to prove itself, in which ads, if any, will be used to prop up the book, in which the book launch will be scheduled, and any book tours. And then if the book doesn't sell huge amounts of copies, it's left to fend for itself.

There are definitely benefits to starting off a book launch with a bang, even if you're self-published. But this bang gets bigger when your number of backlist titles grows. The bang is bigger when you're a bigger name, so don't sweat it too much when you've just started.

Write the next book already.

Rather than rabbit on Facebook, or even run Facebook ads, write the next book.

Rather than fiddle with your current book, write the next book. Make it the second book in your series. Don't start another series; don't start another genre. Write the next book.

There will be time for diversification later.

Don't worry about reviews so much. OK, send your book out to everyone who is a reviewer and wants a copy. Don't be precious about this. Give them the free book. Don't haunt them; just give them the book.

Also ask for reviews from the people on your mailing list. Don't beg; just ask. If someone says they can't afford to buy the book, give it to them if they'll review it. Don't go nuts if they don't end up reviewing. You'll want one less review a lot more than a protracted argument online, or a vengeful bad review because you pissed someone off. Send the book and then let it be, whatever it is that will end up happening.

Write the next book.

If you happen to run a few small promotions and they go well, try to capitalise on it as much as you can, but don't let yourself be distracted that you lose sight of what will drive the sales once the buzz dies down: your next book. (You knew I was going to say that, right?)

There is a saying doing the rounds amongst authors: you're only as good as your last book. If your last book was a year ago, this is going to suppress sales a good deal, because almost all the retailer sites thrive on churn. They want the newest, the best-selling books by the bestselling authors. What's on the front page gets rotated out very quickly. At some sites more quickly than others, but this is the general principle of it. If you haven't released a book in over a year, you can't expect any kind of support from recommendations through retailer sites.

Write the next book. That's what's going to give you the most bang for your buck.

I know it's hard work, but if you want a secret sauce, there it is: write books in a series, place them in a reasonably popular genre, make sure the covers are genre-appropriate, automate your mailing list and then concentrate on the next book. Keep doing this for a few years.

It's called the Three-Year Plan.

Resources

HERE ARE A few things that you might find useful. Visit these sites and use them as jumping points to the vast array of information and community sites that you'll have a hard time finding when you google "self-publishing". Have fun, but remember to keep writing!

Self-publishing identities

I debated citing actual books, but ebooks are changed all the time and advice changes even more quickly. Some of the advice given by people mentioned here is topical and time-sensitive. What works now won't work in six months' time, so I decided that it's better to send you to their websites that contain the latest information.

Joanna Penn

http://www.thecreativepenn.com/

Podcaster, non-fiction and fiction writer. Joanna has a weekly, well-produced podcast that is full of information that relates a lot to building a lasting career. She is one of the veterans of self-publishing and her website is an absolute treasure trove of information.

Mark Dawson

http://selfpublishingformula.com/

Crime author, podcaster and Facebook advertising course provider. I think few people share the boundless enthusiasm, inquisitive and open mind of Mark Dawson. While he does get a bit overly keen with the affiliate linking, he is genuine, the real deal, and he loves sharing. If you ever intend to advertise on Facebook, watch his free videos. He's got a couple of active Facebook communities that are well worth joining.

Nick Stephenson

http://www.blog.yourfirst10kreaders.com/

Author of mysteries and the video course "Your First 10k Readers". Nick perfects the method of recruiting people onto your mailing list. He is the originator of the concept "reader magnet", and provides courses.

Lindsay Buroker

http://lindsayburoker.com/

Few writers are both as laid back and as successful as Lindsay Buroker. Writer of Science Fiction and Fantasy, she is one of those rare creatures who can write a damn good book in a month. And then write another good book the next month, and then two more in the month after that.

Lindsay runs the Science Fiction and Fantasy Marketing podcast with co-hosts Jo Lallo and Jeff Poole. On her website, she writes about her experiences in a comprehensive way.

Yes, there are other people, many of them. I chose the people above because they most closely follow the approach I follow. As an aside, three of them are British. Is that supposed to mean anything?

Other resources

Kindleboards

https://www.kboards.com/index.php/board,60.0.html

The largest community of self-published writers. It may look a bit strange with all the books in people's signatures, but it is the best and most up-to-date open community of writers. You don't even need to be a member to read posts.

Facebook groups Community

The Prosperous Writer Mastermind

https://www.facebook.com/groups/ProsperityforWriters/

Facebook groups Cross-promotion

SF/F Cross-promotion Bulletin Board

https://www.facebook.com/groups/1163390753699773/

Instafreebie promos

https://www.facebook.com/groups/instafreebiepromos/

The Absolute Shoestring Publishing Kit

MANY PEOPLE START publishing without a single red cent to their name. While I would prefer to tell people You Must Invest, I also know and accept that this is not always feasible, and I know of people who have worked themselves out of poverty and bankruptcy using their smarts and an old computer.

So, if you have no money, you probably already know where you can get free word processors and free Internet. I'm going to give you some places where you can get free services that will allow you to publish the best book you can without a budget.

Editing

♦   Workshops

♦   Exchange with friends

Cover design

♦   Ask a friend

♦   Stock art sites, Pixabay

♦   Gimp, Canva

Formatting

♦   D2D

Promotions

♦   Cross-promotions with other authors.

♦   Social media. While it's free, I would absolutely rec-
        ommend against filling up your Twitter and Face-
        book accounts with "Buy My Book!" posts.

Ironically, the best source of free publicity and generating
sales is to give freely. Give your time, promote others, help
others with specific skills you have. Give away free books to
those who are willing to read and review them. Be upfront
about who you are and why you're doing this and why perhaps you can't afford $500 for an editor. Be honest, be open,
be helpful.

The self-publishing community is one that harbours extraor-
dinary generosity. I've been a part of it for six years and have

seen bestselling authors help beginning writers and those beginning writers then go on to help other beginning writers in turn.

When you have a little bit of money, where do you start investing it?

1. If your reviews don't complain too much about errors, spend it on the cover, otherwise editing, or formatting if there is an issue. Or buy Vellum.

2. Buy a domain and website hosting.

3. Get the Instafreebie paid plan to start collecting email subscribers into your as-yet-free account at your email list provider.

4. Go onto that provider's paid plan.

A (Very Limited) Directory Of Recommended Services

THIS IS A very limited list of service providers that I recommend. There is a lot more out there, but these people and companies deliver quality work that I can vouch for.

Editing
EQP Books
Harry DeWulf   http://harrydewulf.com/
Red Adept   http://www.redadeptediting.com/
Polgarus Studio   http://www.polgarusstudio.com/

Cover design
Damonza   http://damonza.com/
Kerry Hynds   http://hyndsstudio.com/
Deranged Doctor   http://www.derangeddoctordesign.com/

Ebooklaunch http://ebooklaunch.com/

Formatting
EQP Books http://eqpbooks.com/
Polgarus Studio http://www.polgarusstudio.com/
Ebooklaunch http://ebooklaunch.com/
Vellum http://vellum.pub/

Mailing lists
Mailerlite http://www.mailerlite.com/
Mailchimp http://mailchimp.com/
SendInBlue http://www.sendinblue.com/

Subscribers
Instafreebie http://www.instafreebie.com/
Bookfunnel http://www.bookfunnel.com/

Promotions
Bookbub http://www.bookbub.com/home/
Ereader News Today http://ereadernewstoday.com/
Freebooksy http://www.freebooksy.com/
Robin Reads http://robinreads.com/

Accounting
Trackerbox http://www.storyboxsoftware.com/
Booktrakr https://www.booktrakr.com/

About The Author

PATTY JANSEN is a writer of fiction and a member of the self-publishing community. Her forum and blog post on the Three-year Plan were the basis for this book. She does not plan to turn this book into courses or seminars on self-publishing. She would rather write.

Patty lives in Sydney, Australia, where she spends most of her time writing Science Fiction and Fantasy. Her story *This Peaceful State of War* placed first in the second quarter of the Writers of the Future contest and was published in their 27th anthology. She has also sold fiction to genre magazines such as Analog Science Fiction and Fact, Redstone SF and Aurealis.

She has written over thirty novels in both the Science Fiction and Fantasy genres, including the *Ambassador* series and the *Icefire Trilogy* and *Moonfire Trilogy*. Her books are available on all ebook outlets as well as in print.

Patty is on Twitter (@pattyjansen), Facebook, LinkedIn, goodreads, LibraryThing, google+ and blogs at: http://patty-jansen.com/.

More By This Author

Quick link to all Patty Jansen's books:
http://pattyjansen.com/pages/quick-overview-of-all-my-books/

In the Earth-Gamra space-opera universe

RETURN OF THE AGHYRIANS
Watcher's Web
Trader's Honour
Soldier's Duty
Heir's Revenge
The Return of the Aghyrians Omnibus

The Far Horizon (For younger readers)

AMBASSADOR
Seeing Red
The Sahara Conspiracy
Raising Hell
Changing Fate
Coming Home
Blue Diamond Sky
The Enemy Within
The Last Frontier
The Alabaster Army

Historical Fantasy

FOR QUEEN AND COUNTRY
Innocence Lost
Willow Witch
The Idiot King
The For Queen and Country Omnibus (Books 1–3)
Fire Wizard
The Dragon Prince
The Necromancer's Daughter

Hard Science Fiction in the ISF-Allion universe
Shifting Reality
Shifting Infinity

Epic, Post-apocalyptic Fantasy

ICEFIRE TRILOGY
Fire & Ice
Dust & Rain
Blood & Tears
The Icefire Trilogy Omnibus

MOONFIRE TRILOGY
Sand & Storm
Sea & Sky
Moon & Earth

Space Agent Jonathan Bartell
Contamination
Observation
Extermination

Short story collections
Out Of Here
New Horizons

Non-Fiction
Self-publishing Unboxed
Mailing Lists Unboxed
Going Wide Unboxed

Visit the author's website at http://pattyjansen.com and register for a newsletter to keep up-to-date with new releases.

22958890R00101

Printed in Poland
by Amazon Fulfillment
Poland Sp. z o.o., Wrocław